YOU ARE NOT ALONE

Personal Stories on Surviving
the Impact of Addiction

YOU ARE NOT ALONE

Personal Stories on Surviving
the Impact of Addiction

Edited by Frances Black

HACHETTE
BOOKS
IRELAND

First published in 2011 by Hachette Books Ireland
Copyright © 2011 The RISE Foundation
Copyright individual contributions © 2001 individual contributor
Copyright Foreword © 2011 Frances Black

1

A CIP catalogue record for this title is available from the British Library.

ISBN 978 1 444 72533 9

Typeset in Baskerville
Typesetting and print design by redrattledesign.com

Printed and bound in Great Britain by CPI Mackays, Chatham ME5 8TD

Hachette Books Ireland policy is to use papers that are natural, renewable and recyclable products and made from wood grown in sustainable forests. The logging and manufacturing processes are expected to conform to the environmental regulations of the country of origin.

The publishers would like to thank:
Mainstream for kind permission to reproduce the excerpt from
The Gambler by Oisín McConville.
Random House Ltd for kind permission to reproduce the excerpt from
Back from the Brink by Paul McGrath.
Jimmy MacCarthy for kind permission to produce the excerpt from
Ride On.

Hachette Books Ireland
8 Castlecourt Centre
Castleknock
Dublin 15
Ireland

A division of Hachette UK Ltd, 338 Euston Road, London NW1 3BH
www.hachette.ie

Contents

I would like to dedicate this book to everyone
out there who has been impacted by addiction,
whether you are in addiction, a family member
with a loved one, or in recovery.

My hope for you is that this book will encourage
you to ask for the support you need and remember:
There is always hope and you are not alone.

Foreword

I set up The RISE Foundation in 2008, inspired by my own journey from addiction to recovery and by my work with families as an addiction therapist in the Rutland Treatment Centre. RISE's goal is simple: to provide support to families who have loved ones in addiction, many of whom are utterly devastated by the consequences of addiction, living in despair or fear and, very often, having lost all hope. We run residential and non-residential Family Programmes, with a team of experienced addiction counsellors.

We are also working on educating people about the impact of addiction. Our eventual goal is to open a dedicated addiction, education and awareness centre on the beautiful Rathlin Island, a haven of peace and serenity. The scenery alone makes you stop in your tracks, forces you to breathe a little deeper. You feel it as soon as you step from the boat onto the land. And the work we do there, with family members who are impacted by addiction, is deeply empowering for everyone involved.

Central to all therapeutic work is the simple sharing of our stories. To share your account with someone – whether it be of your own addiction, or that of a loved one – is the vital first step on the road to recovery, a powerful tool in understanding ourselves and our issues. It opens up the possibility for resolution, however remote that can sometimes seem at first.

Creating a book of these accounts seemed like a natural next step. By reaching out to others, we are saying loudly and clearly to those suffering from the impact of addiction: You are not alone. There are many who understand what you are going through. Help is at hand.

As businessman Ben Dunne says in his inspiring piece on surviving addiction, openness is key to the healing process. Often, it is all too easy to keep our problems bottled up, believing we are protecting ourselves or our loved ones by hiding away feelings of fear and shame. We can convince ourselves that holding on by a bare thread is better than letting go and trusting that our fall will be safely broken. But it is only through openness that we can learn to trust. And only through trust that we can begin to find a way forward – securely and with our true best interests at heart.

The stories contained within these pages are many and varied, as are the addictions they reflect. Some are first-hand accounts by those in recovery. Others are accounts by family members and loved ones. Some, tragically, are accounts of surviving the loss of a loved one. Interspersed between them are my own reflections on some of the key themes central to recovery: the Battle Within, Spirituality, Awareness, Acceptance, Education, Boundaries, Detachment, Forgiveness, True Potential, and Living in the Moment.

I would like to thank each and every contributor for sharing their story so courageously. Although the subject matter contained within them is often unavoidably painful, they are bound together by their courage, honesty, hope and resolve. Each piece seeks in its own way to make peace with a sometimes crazy and chaotic world, where problems have no easy solutions. Each one looks to a brighter day. And, perhaps most importantly, each one recognises that we are not alone.

We are *never* alone.

Frances Black
March 2011

The Battle Within Us

One evening an old Cherokee told his grandson about a battle that goes on inside people. He said, 'My son, the battle is between two wolves inside us all. One is Evil. It is anger, envy, jealousy, sorrow, regret, greed, arrogance, self-pity, guilt, worry, resentment, inferiority, lies, false pride, superiority, and ego. The other is good. It is joy, peace, love, hope, serenity, humility, kindness, benevolence, empathy, humour, generosity, truth, compassion and faith.' The grandson thought for a minute and then asked, his grandfather: 'Which wolf wins?' The old Cherokee simply replied, 'The one you feed.'

Native Amercian metaphor

This simple fable tells us of the battle that goes on within each one of us. The greatest battles that happen in life are not fought on the battlefields; they are fought in our own hearts and souls. We all face conflicts within ourselves, and we often give in to these conflicts

The real enemies these days are forces such as anger, fear, envy, greed, arrogance, guilt, resentment, low self-esteem, lies, superiority, ego and the inability to cope. All of these forces are very prominent when it comes to addiction. When we give in to these negative feelings we lose our power and can become vulnerable. We may act out in an addictive way to escape the reality of how we are feeling, and then become dependent on a substance or behaviour.

If we are a family member of someone in addiction, we may become so preoccupied, worried and anxious about our loved one's behaviour that we end up feeling numb and again lose our power. We think if our loved one is ok, then we are ok; if they are in a bad way, we are in a bad way.

If we can become aware of the battle within us we may discover what we have been running from or trying to avoid. This inner battle between what we know to be right and what we want rages every day, especially for someone in addiction. Every time the person in addiction hits bottom they may vow to never drink again, but when the pain subsides and the haze clears, they are back in the pub or heading down to the off-licence. Addiction is a vicious cycle that often feels impossible to break. To be human is to know what it's like to have this inner conflict raging within us.

What we need to heal ourselves will present itself to us if we allow it. And it is only through this process of healing that we will be able to find and reclaim our lost selves.

Fear can be a very powerful force in our lives. There is healthy fear – this is an awareness and respect for what is dangerous in life. It is what activates our bodies and minds to deal with a threat. It can stop us from doing something dangerous: for example, if a car pulls out in front of us, fear will make us swerve the car to avoid an accident, possibly saving our own lives or someone else's.

Unhealthy fear can be fear of what others will think of us. We can be fearful of not having the comforts of life, and spend our best energies collecting possessions to ensure our comfort. We can be fearful of not feeling loved by someone, and attempt to control them to ensure that we feel loved. We can be fearful of our emotional pain, and use drugs and alcohol to numb ourselves to ensure we don't feel that pain. It is a part of life that we instinctively run from, but working with what we fear most can move us onto the path to healing. Our saving element is within us and is often the last thing we wish to look at or recognise.

When we do, we begin to make peace with ourselves.

Frances

The son of an alcoholic describes how an unexpected correspondence paved the way for him to finally lay to rest the ghosts of a difficult childhood.

The Letter

In October 2003 I received a letter from my father. It was a short note, written in tight, unfamiliar script. In it he said that he knew he had not been a very good father when I was a child. He ended it with an apology.

As I read it, my heart pounded and my stomach ached. It was a bolt out of the blue. Although I saw my father regularly when I visited home to spend time with my mother, I had not talked to him, or even looked at him directly, in nine long years.

The last time I spoke to him, I was screaming into his face while banging the back of his head off the pebbledash wall in the porch of our house. I had never been violent towards another human being, nor have I ever since, and the power of my rage – the uncontrolled expression of it – along with the terror in my father's eyes, all combined to make me sick with fear. Because in that moment, I wanted to kill my father – though now I don't even remember the argument that led to it. To stop myself ever going there again, I vowed that, as far as I was concerned, from that point on, my father did not exist.

Once, during a period when my father wasn't drinking because of ill-health, my mother said that she never fully believed my father was an alcoholic at all. My sister and I, ever in awe at her ability to pretend the problem doesn't exist, gaped open-mouthed at her. 'If he wasn't an alcoholic, then it's worse,' I said. 'He was just a mean bastard.'

I am one of five siblings and my father, who was drunk every day, treated us all in different ways as we were growing up. Although he was often violent to my older and younger brothers, he never hit my sister or me. He virtually ignored the oldest boy and was sometimes nice to the youngest. But one thing was universal – you could never be sure when your time would come to be on the receiving end of his wrath.

We lived in constant fear, tip-toeing through the house in an effort to avoid being set on by him. I remember hiding in dark places when he was in a bad mood, desperately hoping it wasn't my turn to get it in the neck. When it was, the possessions I loved would be destroyed and I'd be called names. 'Fairy', 'queer', 'bender' – these were favourites, as I was a camp little boy with artistic leanings. Most days I was branded a 'waster', a 'waste of space', and 'a nothing'. My father railed at heaven for having been cursed with such terrible children and his anger underpinned every waking moment of our lives.

My sister and I would cry in my bedroom listening to the screams of our brother being beaten up. Afterwards, when we went to comfort him, my father would intervene and bitterly tell us to 'fuck off'.

We would listen to my mother and father fighting downstairs, wondering if and when he would punch her, or whether she would storm out of the house, get into the car and drive away into the night. If she did the latter, I would wait fearfully in the dark, praying that she would not be killed in a crash, that she would come home safely to us.

When I wasn't trying to stay out of his sight, I went out of my way to gain his love and approval. Learning the piano, I strived to play jazz because that was his favourite music. I played in the hope that he might tell me I was doing well, but praise never came. As I grew up, this craving for praise never left me. As a young adult, I would find myself doing little things to make him love me. Cleaning the house, taping his favourite TV show, making a cup of coffee, and buying him a little present. But his love and approval didn't come.

My mother's consistency is what saved me, I think. Even though she was driven to co-dependent dementia by my father's drinking and his anger, eking out a secret life of poverty behind closed doors in our middle-class Cork neighbourhood, she never lost a chance to overtly love and praise her children. When I was eight I wrote a song and she told me it was good enough to win the Eurovision. I fully believed her. I performed it in a concert and she told me she couldn't have been prouder. But for her, I would have grown up without a centre to myself, without ground to stand on.

Of his five children, I was the only one to receive a letter from our father. A huge part of me was outraged at this injustice and wanted to return it to him, telling him I never wanted to hear from him again. But something told me to wait. After sitting with the letter for a month or so, I wrote a paragraph back saying that I was confused by the feelings the letter brought out in me and that we would have to wait and see how things panned out.

The moment I posted that letter was the moment I grew up. I had written to him as an adult, expressing myself for the first time as his equal. I told the truth, to him and to myself, without drama. I wasn't reacting to him or trying to make him love me. I was simply being myself, without fear, without shame and without anger.

My father and I talk to each other now, generally about the weather. There are no heart-to-hearts or great moments of love between us, and his drunken behaviour still annoys the hell out of me. But I tell him so without disproportionate rage. He accepts it and shuts up. Sometimes I catch him looking at me and I know that he's afraid he'll lose this shred of a relationship that he's salvaged from the wreckage. That's his fear. It belongs to him and I don't share it.

There are scars from growing up in an alcoholic home that will never leave me, horrible insecurities that rise to the surface every now and then in my relationships, especially a fear of being blind-sided when things are going well. But the biggest scar has healed. I have learned that I am not a waste of space or 'a nothing'.

My father's letter might not have said 'I love you' or 'I am proud of you', but in receiving it and replying to it, I found the space to love and be proud of myself. It gave me an opportunity to end my messed-up relationship with him and start something new, on my own terms. It allowed me to break free of the scared child, still hiding in the dark.

With support, a mother comes to understand her son's addiction, and learns that the only way to enable his recovery is to take a step back.

Dear Son

It only seems like yesterday that you were my little boy, always busy making things and fixing bikes. You were a little messer and known by everyone on the street as 'the little daredevil'. You spent more time in Temple Street following your little stunts on that BMX bike, but behind the little tough guy was the softest, kindest heart. Many a morning you would pretend to forget something just so that you could come back and give me a hug before you left for school.

You were very bright in school and I was so proud when you did so well in your life and job. You seemed so happy. To this day I still can't believe how quickly things were to change. But I've learned that's what addiction can do to the best of people. Slowly but surely it took the fun-loving, kind son I knew away.

You became a stranger to me. I just did not know what to do to help you. I made lots of mistakes thinking that I could fix your problems, bailing you out with loans, making excuses for your actions, but in hindsight I was only making the problem worse.

I will never forget the fear I felt when I'd get the calls to say you were in A & E or lying on a road somewhere. The huge shame I felt when I saw the state you were in, lying on a bed that should have been there for some sick or elderly person.

Or the devastation I felt when I tried to be tough with you and you would threaten to end it all. The worry, the hurt, the pain I felt was unbearable at times.

I sat with you for hours while you cried and went through withdrawal. I believed your promises, only to be heartbroken when you'd go out and do it all over again.

I tried to help you by getting tablets from the doctor, believing that you really needed them. But, of course, that didn't help. It caused so many rows and disagreements in the family. Your brothers and sisters could see that this was killing me and it was beginning to affect the whole family.

When I first sought help, I was so happy. I went along to the RISE group and it was the best thing I ever did – it gave me hope. I had blamed myself for everything. But I met other people who were in the same situation as me, who could understand what I was going through. I was not alone. I truly believe that the support I got has helped to get you into recovery today. When I got stronger, so did you.

I began to accept that I was powerless and prayed that you would use some of the skills you learned over the years to get better. I'd pray that you would use the stubborn streak that you had as a young boy to beat this addiction.

It gave me the strength to realise and accept that I was enabling you to continue with your addiction. When I was bailing you out I was only helping you to kill yourself.

You are doing well now, thank God. Sober and working

today. The son I knew has re-emerged. I am very thankful for that.

Always remember that I still love you and I am proud of you and all that you have achieved. I know that you have lost a lot and each day must be a struggle.

I am glad that you have learned to laugh again. When you said to me recently that you have laughed more in the last month than you had in the last three years, it made me feel so happy for you.

For me that's a blessing.

Love,
Mam

Last Chance This Life

When he was six, and the shadows grew long
I'd call him home from play,
'Last chance for the slide, and the swings, my son,
last chance today.'

Then he was fifteen, and drinking too much,
hanging with his peers,
'It's June, best get your schoolwork done,
last chance this year.'

Now he's fifty, with lungs turned to stone
since he took Lady Crack for his wife,
'So much is gone, son, but you can recover.
Last chance this life.'

Terry Barker
www.lastchancethislife.com

Excerpt from 'The Gambler' by Oisín McConville

By the time we won the All Ireland in 2002, gambling was already a huge and destructive part of my life. When I wasn't training and signing jerseys in the phone shop and smiling for the cameras, I was hiding away in some dark corner of a bookies, alone with a docket like all the other loners in such places. I had no real bills at that time. Everything I earned was going into my pocket on a Friday, in the form of a cheque, but it was quickly cashed and by the time the doors were locked and another week's work was done I'd already have placed my first bet. An hour later, all that work could have been for nothing and I wouldn't have enough money to get a sandwich on the way back to Cross. If people had known the truth, they wouldn't have come looking for autographs and signatures. I was a dark, lonely, depressed individual away from all the supposed glamour. I never played football for that, though; I played it to run and hide from my real self for just a few hours on a Sunday.

I regularly asked myself if I could quit and the answer was always the same: of course I could and I would when things started getting serious but at that moment it was just a bit of fun. I was lying to myself. I was already in too deep to escape but I saw it as a bad habit and no more. I was completely blind to the reality.

After that, there was no real time frame. I can't tell you how much I lost on a certain day or month, or in a year. I don't know when the bad days were and I'm not so sure where there were any good days. I just know that the next seven years were a block of wasted time that could have been the end of me.

In the beginning, I would be annoyed when leaving a bookies after losing money. By the end, I was lying on a bed in an apartment I had rented in Cavan just down the road from the pub, curtains closed to the outside world, depression eating into me and the odd thought of ending it all going through my mind because I had long since closed every door with an exit sign above it.

There was one day that I walked into a bookies with £6,000 and my last bet before leaving was £3. That's how low it can take you. Anyone with a problem could find themselves in that position but anyone with self-respect would walk away, realising their day was done. Not me.

I was clearly at sea but nobody can help you in that situation because you've become a complete loner. You're in a world of your own. Nobody can get in on you. Your world is filled with the same faces, the same loners, and you look over the odd time and feel sorry for them, but you're one of them and soon enough there's another race, another bet, another step deeper into the river of trouble that can sweep your life away from you.

I was borrowing money from acquaintances, borrowing money from banks, so I could go and give the big time another shot. I was even selling a few bits and pieces that I had, expecting to win a fortune. But, of course, you never do and the money always ends up on the other side of the counter. Gambling is a game where the opposition always wins.

I kept it deep inside me and I'd stay there for hours thinking about the situation, realising how stupid I had been and how there was no way out. I couldn't tell and I couldn't get the money together. With no way out, what do you do? It's then you begin to think about doing something stupid. I don't think I'd ever have gone through with it but suicide crossed my mind as the easiest solution to all of this on more than a handful of occasions. There were many times when I thought it would be a lot easier not to be around to see the man I had become when he got a little further down the tracks.

My brothers asked me one day about what I had been at. There was an outstanding bill from a cash and carry and they were pressing me about this and all the other bills that had been coming to my mother's house, asking me about any problems I might have.

I sat in the back of my brother's car as he asked questions and I just broke down. I told him everything. He said he knew I was in debt but they all wanted me to come clean and admit what was going on.

When I first walked in the door I wanted to run as far as possible. It's a place where alcoholics dry out and they were everywhere, and looking at them I was wondering how this was going to be of any use to me. I just wanted to meet someone, one of the nurses, and ask if this would do any good to me, someone that's gambling. When I did get my chance, they all said the same thing to me: it's not the same addiction but it's the same principle. There was always a few drinking and doing drugs, making sure they never recovered.

At first, when I came out, if you asked me my thoughts

on it all, I would have said I just wasted three months of my life, but I guess it had to be done and I had nobody else to blame but myself. It's only now I'm realising that they were the best and most important three months of my life and always will be. Better than an Ulster or an All Ireland or any of that, because now I can enjoy life when I walk back over the white line. It's three months I put into my life rather than it being taken away.

A sister recounts to her brother how his addiction has affected her life.

Dear Brother

I thought I was going to lose my mind, I had so many emotions all mixed up in my head: hurt, fear, shame, guilt, anger, all in one day. Sometimes, all in one hour. When I was alone in the house, or in the car, I'd actually practice conversations out loud that I wanted to have with you. Tactics I was going to use to make you stop. I would carefully choose the words, because I thought that if I could only find the right words to say to you, you'd cop on and maybe you'd listen. Then I'd get so upset. I had to pull the car over to the side of the road many times to pull myself together.

I dreaded the phone ringing; the calls could come anytime, day or night, no matter where I was. You've been found unconscious; you're on your way to the hospital; you've been arrested; you've been beaten up; you've crashed the car; you're threatening to kill yourself; you're lying on the floor and they can't get into the house; you're missing. You'd sometimes go missing for days – it was torture. I'd drive to places we used to go as kids, looking up at the trees looking for your body. You had told me so many times that you just wanted to die but did not want to do it in the house. I had convinced myself that you would hang yourself in an isolated place.

I'd put on a brave face in front of my husband and child, or so I thought, but it showed itself in other ways. I'd become impatient, distant, nervous, snappy, withdrawn from friends. I couldn't mention your name in our house anymore because my husband would become annoyed. He couldn't understand why I just could not accept that what you were doing was your choice. Of course, I felt hurt that my husband could not empathise and support me, but he had his own problems and I was so consumed with you that I failed to even notice.

I just couldn't focus on anything. I felt so sick, with real pains – headaches, stiffness in my neck, unbearable stomach pain that would just not go away. A constant ache.

I'd wake up tired in the mornings, remembering the horrifying thoughts from my dreams the night before – visions of you lying dead in the church, or you sitting crying somewhere alone.

It's heartbreaking to watch a loved one in addiction changing so dramatically in front of your eyes. The whole family was affected. We were all close – meeting up used to be great fun, we were very comfortable in each other's company. But now there was a horrible feeling in the house when we were together. Our mother was devastated, she literally aged overnight. Discussions about you would end in angry disagreements. We all had our opinions of how to deal with it and this sometimes led to tensions between us, especially with Mam. She found it hard to let go, to say no to you.

She would get annoyed at us because maybe we seemed to be 'too hard', 'not tolerant' or 'not helpful' enough. We'd suggested many forms of treatments: more treatment centres; sending you away; having you locked up in a mental hospital; beating you up; blanking you from our family, or just leaving you to do what ever you wanted to do.

But, of course, it's not that easy when your mother's heart is broken and you just can't see any light at the end of the tunnel. There was just a feeling of total despair and powerlessness. I often thought that you would be better off dead, especially when we were getting the suicide threats. I was consumed with guilt afterwards and was afraid to reveal these thoughts to anyone in case they thought I was some sort of monster. How could a woman, a sister, a mother think like that?

Thank God I saw the interview about The RISE Foundation on TV one morning. I cried my eyes out when I heard that there was help for families. At last I could at least try and get some help for our mother! Up until this time I had been constantly trying to get help for you and no matter what I did it hadn't worked.

I decided to attend the programme to 'support Mam' – it was the best thing I ever did. At that point I didn't realise how much help I needed myself. I can't begin to explain how much it changed my life. The programme empowered me to make changes to my own life. I now realise that I made some mistakes along the way too. I learned new skills to help me cope with my feelings towards you. Slowly I felt the weight of guilt, fear, loss, anger, distrust, resentment, shame and powerlessness lift from me.

It was an unbelievable relief to speak to people who

understood what it felt like and know that I would not be judged. I've learned to verbalise how I feel about what you're doing rather than what I think you should be doing. I've learned to accept and cope. I'm glad that I can now have civilised conversations with you. You know I still worry about you. But always remember that I love you very very much and will be there for you through recovery if you need me. I've learned to laugh again. To enjoy my own family and not feel guilty about that. I hope some day that you can do the same.

It's a long road ahead for all of us but I find that each day it gets a little easier.

Your loving sister

*A young woman thanks a treasured friend
for being there in a time of need.*

Dear Friend

Thanks for talking to me today.

It's good to speak to someone who understands the way I'm feeling right now.

I've been scared to reveal my true feelings to anyone in case they might judge me. I'm not a horrible person and I don't like the thoughts that are going through my head. But I can't help the emotions that come naturally to me.

How could I not feel any sadness when I heard that he was very sick in hospital? So he might die. I hung up the phone and just thought ok, so that's going to be a big inconvenience and expense for me – having to return home from the US to Ireland.

I didn't cry for him, I wasn't sad for him, I didn't feel any loss. How could I? He made my childhood hell. He was the reason I ended up over here alone. I ran away from the pain and hurt but, of course, it followed me – I wasn't going to escape that easy.

I still have all the memories of every single fight, every terrifying instance, every embarrassing moment, every tear I cried. How can I forget? You would think that after so many years I would have been able to let go of all those feelings and memories – but I can't.

Al-Anon helped me out a lot over here through the years

but it's still moments like this that drag up the deepest memories and horrible feelings – it hurts so much I find it hard to breathe.

It's good to have someone to talk to.

Love,
Your forever thankful friend x

Bursting with pride, a mother tells her daughter, who is in recovery from addiction, how delighted she is at all the positive changes she is making in her life.

Dear Joan

You're doing so well. I am very proud of what you have achieved and how bravely you have fought to escape from the hell you were living in. I understand it wasn't easy for you, and how difficult it was to walk away from the one thing that remained with you when you had lost everything else.

You look so healthy and clean, it's hard to believe that you're the same girl I saw curled up in a heap with sadness and fear in her eyes on that cold October day last year. Your hair is all shiny and styled now, and that new make-up you bought brings out the best features on your lovely face. It's great to see you smile and to hear your laughter again.

The kids look great too – they're enjoying every minute of having their mammy back in their lives. Does it feel great to have their little arms around your neck like that again and their little kisses on your cheek? They love the stories you tell them at night before you tuck them in. I can hear the happiness in their voices when they speak to me on the phone – all full of news for their granny.

How's college going? When you were little, you always

said that you wanted to be a nurse. I said to your dad that you would make a great nurse because you were always such a caring child. Either a nurse or a vet because you were always bringing home stray cats and dogs and little birds that fell from their nests. Do you remember the little funerals we'd hold for the ones that didn't make it?

It's great to see that you've set yourself some goals and that you're thinking about the future with such a positive outlook. You're still only young, love, and you have such a long future ahead of you.

I met Nancy the other day, and she's still the same – a nosy ol' busybody as always. Anyhow, she was asking me how you were. My heart nearly burst with pride when I told her that you're 'attending Trinity College now' in my nicest voice! She almost looked disappointed with the news and well, I can tell you, I felt great for the whole day – it was like a tonic.

I love you so much sweetheart. Keep strong and take care.

Your loving mother

A grown-up son tries to make sense of the feelings of loss and abandonment he still experiences, in a letter to his mother in addiction.

Dear Mother

My youngest memories were pretty good; I remember the times that we were all together. I know it wasn't perfect – I remember the problems with Da's drinking, and how he caused trouble at home.

But we had a home, we were a family, I felt secure and I felt loved – that's all I needed back then.

I'm trying to figure out when it started to go wrong. I know you were depressed, and when Dad died I know it was hard on you – but we needed you more than ever.

I needed you to be strong. But you found a new love – one that did not include us.

For years, I have asked the same questions over and over in my head:

Why did you abandon your family?

Why did you abandon me?

What did I do wrong to make you do this?

Did you not care about us?

Did you ever think about us in your sober moments?

Do you ever think about us in your sober moments now?

Do you look back with hurt and pain and loss, like I do?

I was only 9 years old when you abandoned us and

we became homeless. Although I was raised by a loving foster mother, nothing or no one was able to take the place of the parents I should have had. I lost both my parents – my real mother died a long long time ago, savaged by depression, alcohol and drugs.

The person standing before me now is a stranger.

Your son

Frances Black of The RISE Foundation writes about how she finally faced her demons and set out on her true path. She was inspired to write this letter after hearing a Hazelden lecture on 'Slick: The Voice of Addiction'.

Dear Slick

So, how are you doing? You know, in a funny sort of a way, I have a kind of respect for you. Even though there were times when I was extremely angry with you for all the pain that you had caused in my life. Thankfully, I don't feel angry with you anymore. I think that's because I have a good understanding now as to what you are all about. We have a fair few memories together, don't we?

Looking back now, I think you were always kind of hovering around me, even as a young child. Waiting . . .

From early on, I remember always having this empty feeling inside, a lost feeling of never quite fitting in. In primary school, even though I had friends, I always felt somehow disconnected, different to the other kids. I had a nun in third class who beat it into me that I was stupid because I couldn't understand the maths, and that belief stuck with me for many years. As I went into secondary at the age of 12, that feeling of emptiness intensified. I struggled with shyness. When the teacher told me that I had to repeat first year because I was too young, I was devastated. I couldn't hear the 'too young' part, all I took from it was that that I was too stupid to move forward. I often wonder if that was your voice, Slick, that voice that used to constantly tell me that I was useless, ugly, fat, and, of course, stupid.

When I was 13, I discovered alcohol, and I will never ever forget the feeling I got when I drank that first bottle of ale. I didn't like the taste, so I put lemonade in it to dampen it. But that warm feeling it gave me, the emptiness that it filled . . . I thought all my prayers had been answered. Slick, you had been waiting a long time for that moment. At last you had me, as this marked the beginning of my very dysfunctional relationship with alcohol. Throughout my teenage years I would always drink more than my friends. They would go home but I would want to stay drinking. Somehow I managed to get through those years, although I have to say there were a few dodgy moments.

I am sure you remember the night when I was 17, when I drank so much that I nearly killed myself. I don't remember much of it, as I was in a state of blackout. I was told that I went into the sitting room in our big old house in Charlemont Street, locked the door and switched on the gas fire but didn't light it. My mother smelled the gas and kicked in the door. When she saw I was unconscious, she dragged me down the stairs and got me out into the back yard, where I came to. I know that not in my wildest dreams would I have done that if I hadn't had alcohol on me. When my mother told me the next day what had happened, I was shocked and horrified. It was never again spoken about or mentioned in our house.

I am very aware that, had my mother not found me, this would have been your final triumph, Slick. Thankfully you didn't succeed. I now know that for you, at the end of the day, death is the ultimate prize.

Somehow I managed to get through my twenties relatively intact. Though by the time I was 26, I had a broken marriage behind me. Being alone and so young, with two small children, was a difficult time for me, and you were still hovering around . . . Waiting . . .

That was when I started to drink the bottle of wine every night, sometimes two. I would open the bottle at around six in the evening and would continue drinking until I fell asleep. I really hated the power you had over me then; I wanted to stop so badly and tried so many times. Somehow, I would hear that voice saying things like, 'Ah, sure it's only wine', 'It's no big deal, you are not hurting anyone', or 'You need it to get some sleep'. The turning point came one night as I was sitting watching telly. It was as if things around me started happening in slow motion. I kept staring at the glass of wine I was holding. I asked myself, 'Why am I drinking this? I don't want it.' But I couldn't put the drink down. I just had to finish that second bottle of wine.

I knew then that I was in trouble, that I needed help, but that I couldn't do it on my own. Thank God for that journalist who wrote the article in *The Irish Times* . . . I don't recall her name. But she had an almost identical drinking pattern to me. She had got in touch with a place called Stanhope Street, where they had an outpatient treatment centre for anyone who had an alcohol problem. The phone number was at the end of the page, and it took every bit of courage I had to call them to make the appointment.

That was the beginning of an amazing journey for me. I attended Stanhope Street three nights a week for a year. My mam was a wonderful support to me at that time, and I couldn't have done it without her. She would babysit for me those nights, and she never asked me any questions; she just accepted me and the situation and took it all in her stride. With a lot of support from Stanhope Street, I stopped drinking and my singing career took off, but you were still close by Slick, waiting for the next opportunity to pounce, always waiting . . .

I am not so sure that you were too happy with the situation, Slick. I had stopped drinking, I had met Brian, a lovely Cork man, and we had bought our first home together. The children were happy; I had made my first solo album which went to number one, and I started to win awards for my music. Yet when I look back on that time, I feel sad. I wish I could have truly appreciated all the incredible things that were happening in my life. But unfortunately there was always that negative voice present within me, telling me I didn't deserve it, that I wasn't worthy of the success. I kept thinking, people will realise that I am not really a good singer, that I am a fake. I felt so unworthy that I put the awards I had won away in a box in the attic. And the guilt! I was aware that there were people out there who were really struggling with life, who had problems a hundred times worse than mine. But I couldn't stop the way I was feeling.

It was around this time that I hit my first real rock bottom. Unable to function, I even cancelled a UK tour. I knew I needed help. I went to doctors, psychiatrists, hypnotists, even psychics looking for help. I was prescribed tablets, but they didn't work for me. I wasn't aware then that I needed support and guidance from other people like me – people who had stopped drinking, but who, unlike me, had learned the tools to cope with their new reality.

Through a series of 'coincidental' events and a wonderful doctor called Patrick Nugent (who has passed away since), I found myself going in through the doors of AA ten years after first attending Stanhope Street. It took me that length of time to realise that I couldn't do it my way anymore. I believe this was the first time that I truly accepted that I was an alcoholic. And it was there that I met the most amazing people imaginable. They were wonderfully humble, spiritual and giving people. At last I was not on my own and I took on board the guidance I got from them.

So, Slick, you shrivelled away again for another while. I began to get my power back and feel ok again. I still struggled with the negative voice but it was a little more manageable. I continued gigging and, for the first time, I was really enjoying it. I was so appreciative of my work and of those people who continued to come and see me perform. I travelled to the States, England, Holland and I performed in theatres the length and breadth of Ireland, always finishing in the best theatre of all, the Olympia. Each and every time I played the Olympia, it felt like I had died and gone to heaven. Playing there was living the dream for me. The Olympia theatre will always have a very special place in my heart. But it wasn't over for you, Slick, was it? You were still there, still waiting . . .

A few years passed and life was good, until my Mam got sick. What a brilliant woman she was. Born Pattie Daly, off Cork Street in Dublin, Mam was a Liberties' woman and proud of it. She had a tough life, as did many of the women of her generation, and when we were kids, I often remember her worrying about where she would get the few bob needed to put dinner on the table for her brood of five. I always saw her as a strong, independent, determined woman. I lived next door to her in latter years and she was a great support to me in every way, never more so than with my children. She was brilliant with all of her grandchildren and loved them all so much.

Mam was well into her eighties when her health started to go downhill and she became more dependent on us all. She needed a lot of minding, and between myself and my sister Mary, we did our best to take care of her. But there was huge sadness for us both, especially when we started to lose her to dementia. It was around this time that I eased off going to AA meetings, which I know now is a dangerous warning sign. My excuse was that I was tired, busy and had other priorities, but believe me, they were just excuses. Slick, you were moving closer to me, and I was slipping back into my old ways, feeling low, exhausted and, again, unworthy.

When I went to the doctor to tell him how tired I was feeling, he diagnosed me with depression and put me on antidepressants, but he also suggested I take sleeping tablets to deal with my insomnia. I was pretty naive at the time, totally unaware that I could get addicted to them. Slick, you crept back into my life in such an insidious and sly way that I didn't even see you coming, and soon you were back in full swing again.

The sleepers numbed out the feeling of powerlessness I felt around Mam being sick. Initially, I would fall asleep on them, but soon I was becoming immune to their effects. I would take them at ten o'clock at night, but not fall asleep until much later on. I began taking them earlier, first at 9.00 p.m., then 8 p.m. I loved the feeling they gave me, the way they numbed the pain. But the funny thing was that now I could function quite normally on them. After taking them, I could still take care of Mam, dress her for bed and make her supper, and I just felt normal.

The dark side was that when I'd wake up the following morning, feeling more exhausted than ever and with no motivation to get through the day, I became preoccupied with the tablets and when I was going to take them. I would look forward to eight o'clock coming. Then one day I thought, why wait until eight? Why not take them a bit earlier? I had started on the tablets in June 2002. It was now only September, and I was totally dependent. It was the beginning of the end.

I was going to different doctors to get prescriptions to keep me going. It was all a bit of a haze, really. I was recording an album at the time but I had absolutely no interest in it and ended up putting it on hold. I kept a very low profile. I was somehow able to function at home. I think my husband Brian put it down to me being depressed.

Then, one Friday in October, it all came to a head. Thankfully the kids were both away at the time. I must have taken a fair few tablets that day, because Brian noticed that I was acting strange. He challenged me on it and we ended up having a row. I don't remember much about it, as I now believe that I was in a blackout, but I was told that I had opened up a two litre bottle of wine and started drinking it. It must have broken Brian's heart to see me in this state after being 14 years off alcohol. Slick, you really got me this time . . . I was so sick that night. I don't remember falling asleep but I will never ever forget the feeling when I woke up. The sense of shame was enormous, about what I had done, the heartache and disappointment that I must have caused Brian. I didn't know what to do. Brian came and sat at the side of the bed and said that he was very concerned about me and had made a few calls. He then asked if I would be willing to go into a residential treatment centre.

I immediately said yes. Then I started to think about it all. What would my children think of me? They were both young adults now. How could I tell them that I was taking sleeping tablets and had been drinking again? I wondered what I would tell my family. Would they be ashamed of me? What would I tell my friends? What about my Irish tour that I was about to embark on? How would we explain to all those people that the gigs were cancelled? The fear and the shame kicked in big time, but in my heart I knew this was the only way forward, not just for me but for Brian and my two lovely children. I couldn't do this to them anymore and I had to get it sorted once and for all. So the decision was made. I was going to Talbot Grove Treatment Centre in Castleisland, County Kerry, the following day: Sunday, 27 October 2002

I will never forget the drive down. It was late afternoon when we left, on a cold, wet, miserable evening. I felt really scared not knowing what to expect, but mostly I just felt the deep shame of letting Brian and the children down. I couldn't believe that I had let it go so far, that I gave you, Slick, my power. I had let you win and I felt broken.

Walking in through the doors of the old Rectory building that was now a treatment centre was one of the most difficult and scary things I ever had to do in my life. But I have no doubt that it was the best thing I have ever done. It was a fantastic experience. What I learned in there about addiction was phenomenal. It was there that I first heard the lecture on you, Slick, 'the voice of addiction'. It made so much sense to me. I met fantastic people. The counsellors were brilliant and understood exactly what was going on. Best of all, there was no judgement. No one thought badly of me, they just said that I had an illness that I had the power to recover from, if I really wanted to. And they gave me the tools to do it.

So, Slick, I left Talbot Grove, fully determined that I would never give you my power again. I made a commitment then to myself that I would do everything that I possibly could not to let my family down again. Always remembering that I could only do that one day at a time. Talbot Grove had put me in touch with the

Rutland Treatment Centre in Rathfarnam. This is where I would be attending my aftercare programme, which I have to say was absolutely fantastic and again life-changing. I connected in with all the supports that were suggested. I was on a wonderful journey of recovery.

Thankfully Mam was unaware that I had been down in Talbot Grove. I made the decision not to tell her, as she was getting more and more confused, and I felt it would have been hard for her to understand. That Christmas of 2002, she had a bad fall and ended up with a broken shoulder. By this stage, we knew that she needed more nursing help than we could give her at home, and the heartbreaking decision was made by the family that she would go into a nursing home. She went in to St John's in Sandymount in January 2003 and, sadly, she passed away on the 25 October the same year.

I was and still am so grateful to have been clean and sober for that final year of my Mam's life. I visited her every single day, except when I was away gigging, and I have so many good memories of the time we spent together. Sometimes we would sit together in her room and, even though she might not be able to talk to me, I would just chat away to her and tell her how everyone was doing. Other times, when she was in good form, we would sing all her old songs together. Even though she couldn't really talk anymore, she could still sing the old songs.

The month before she died, while we were sitting together, I looked at her with a sense of sadness, as she was so weak and feeble-looking. I bent down and whispered in her ear, 'Mam, I love you.' She turned and looked straight into my eyes. 'I love you, too,' she said. I had never heard my mam saying those words, we weren't that type of family. So I cried tears of joy that day and, once again, felt unbelievable gratitude to be sober.

So, as a legacy to my mother's memory, I decided to go back to college. I wanted to learn every possible thing I could about addiction, as I believe knowledge is power. This was a scary decision for me as I still held the deep-seated belief that I wouldn't be able to learn. The negative voice was saying, 'Who do you think you are, going back to college, sure weren't you told in school that you were stupid?' But although the voice was constant, this time I refused to listen, this time I rose above it, this time I held my head high. I walked in through the doors of the ATI Institute out in All Hallows and I was determined that I would succeed and that someday I would be an addiction counsellor and I would help other people just like me, and their families.

So, that's my story of my journey to recovery. Slick, I am aware that you are still hovering around, always waiting. But you are not going to get me today. I am clean and sober today and I intend to stay that way. I became that addiction counsellor; I trained in the Rutland treatment centre and I then went on to work there. After a few years I left and I am now founder of an organisation called The RISE Foundation. It is an organisation that supports families who have loved ones in addiction. I have a first-class team of people around me who support me. Myself and Stephen Rowen run ten-week programmes and residential programmes for families who want to learn about addiction.

I am still singing and performing and I hope to bring out another album soon. Myself, Brian and the kids have never been happier and I can safely say that I feel so lucky to be living a life beyond my wildest dreams.

And lastly I just want to say . . .

Mam, I hope I have made you proud. ☺

Slán go fóill,
Frances

Spirituality

'If you want to accomplish the goals of your life,
You have to begin with the spirit.'

Oprah Winfrey

Sometimes we may hear addiction being described as 'a soul sickness', or we may hear the term 'the hole in the soul', or 'the yearning void'. Years of taking a substance or acting out in addictive behaviour can take its toll and make us so sick inside, whether it is spiritually, mentally, emotionally or physically. The emotions experienced by the person in addiction and the family member are almost identical. Addiction can cause deep anxiety, sleepless nights and sometimes even physical illness. Feelings of confusion, fear, and shame can be overwhelming.

For those in addiction, life is thrown off balance. Their bodies grow sick. They often find themselves unable to perform at work or school. Social contacts may disappear. Finally, they become more and more isolated and disconnected from their loved ones and the world around them.

For the family member, the emotional distress they suffer is often compounded by the belief that they somehow caused or contributed to their loved one's addiction, or that they could have done something to prevent it. They also often experience similar side effects in their personal life as the person in addiction. All of these feelings can be soul destroying for both the person in addiction and the family member.

According to *The Big Book of Alcoholics Anonymous*, addiction is a spiritual dis-ease, or a soul sickness. One of most tragic consequences of an addictive situation is the way it can destroy the heart and soul of a beautiful person and their family. A spiritual emptiness can be felt by both parties. We all have the ability to connect with the soul or spirit of others; we can do this through talking, music, poetry and many other ways. It is these deeper relationships that the person in addiction and the family member desperately need. Because addiction is a direct assault against the self, it is also a direct attack on the spirit or soul of the person suffering from the addiction and the spirits of their family members. Our spirit nourishes life; addiction leads to spiritual death. Therefore, stepping into recovery can be tough, but is essential if you want a better life.

If you feel you may have a problem, or that someone you love has a problem, decide if you're willing to do whatever it takes to succeed at recovery. Be ready and willing to change. Connect with a support group that suits you, whichever one best serves your needs. This support and fellowship is vital. Recovery is about realising that, alone, we are powerless to solve the problem. To get the strength we need to recover, we have to admit that we need help from something greater than ourselves. Addiction is an example of extreme self-will, but we all struggle with self-will, attachment, expectations and resentments. That's why addiction is often used as a metaphor for the struggle of life.

Frances

A young woman writes to her younger brother about his long battle with alcohol addiction.

Dear little brother

Over the years, I have watched your life spiral downward because of your abuse of alcohol and drugs. Every time you drank or did drugs, you became a stranger – someone I didn't know or like – with such rage and anger that your own siblings and parents were terrified of you. I couldn't understand why you would repeatedly do this to yourself over and over again. But I had to come to realise that it wasn't a choice you were making – it was an addiction for you.

My fondest memory of you was holding you in my seven-year-old arms on the swing out back and singing to you – a sweet little baby in my arms. I used to run home from school and grab you out of your pram, running out to the back garden so that I could swing you and make you feel safe. It made me feel safe too. It took us both to another world – away from the fear that surrounded us. I wished so many times over the years that I could go back to that moment: grab you out of your addiction, hold you in my arms and swing you on the swing, singing soft lullabies and making you feel safe. I think that the most frustrating part for me was not being able to stop you from destroying yourself, not being able to hold you in my arms again and say, 'It's okay, I've got you, you're safe now.' Instead, I had to stand on the sidelines and watch you spiral downward, affecting everyone around you with your violent outbursts and your lack of self-control.

There were times over the years when you seemed like you were getting it together — you'd stop drinking and everything would calm down. All of us in the family, your friends too, would hold our breaths — not quite able to relax fully, but hoping and praying that maybe this time you had stopped for good. Then there would be another outburst. Something would set you off, something somebody said that made you angry, hurt your feelings. That was all it took to give you an excuse to go on a binge. Mam would wait up at night, unable to sleep until she knew you were safely home, but, at the same time, afraid that a huge fight would break out when you arrived. Our little brother, the baby of the family, used to lie awake at night calling to Mam: 'Is he home yet?' He worried about you, probably more than any of us. I saw that little boy age before my eyes, the stress on his face wondering where his big brother was, wondering if you would ever come home again, afraid of what would happen once you got there. He never saw fault in you, he only looked up to you and saw no wrong in anything you did — until the day you turned on him. That was the day you lost his respect and admiration.

The others in the family got so annoyed at your behaviour. But I always held out hope for you. There was a bond between us that had been formed all those years ago on that swing out the back. My arms always felt like they were holding you — even though I was now thousands of miles away, living my own life. I prayed for you so much over the years. I had to believe, somewhere deep inside me, that there was a flicker of life in you, some part of you that wanted to fight through your addiction and grab onto your life.

Mam always stood up for you. She would tell me of another incident and beg me not to say anything to the others, knowing that they would give up, and glad that I would say another prayer for you. I saw you as a tortured soul, someone who was in so much pain that they needed to constantly escape into a world of drunken bliss, so as not to have to face the anguish and pain of their lives. It was such a helpless feeling, watching you self-destruct and not being able to stop you. But when a person is going through something like that, they have to be the ones to fight. Nobody can fight the battle for you – we can only stand by your side and hold your hand, and be there when you fall. I tried to be there as much as I could, taking all your phone calls, being patient with you, even though nothing you said made sense to me.

I remember Mam telling me about the day she believed something clicked in your head. It was a conversation you and she had about the past; how you had always felt that you were unloved, that you always felt you were left on the sidelines, and how in the past she had always made excuses and said that you were being ridiculous, feeling like that. For the first time in your life, she said that she was sorry – you had been validated finally – and she told you that she loved you. It changed something inside your heart. Even after years of trying to regain control of your life, going through rehab several times, nothing had clicked in your mind until the day your own mother validated the hurt you had felt about being neglected and unloved as a child. It was then that we began to see a change.

Suddenly you had purpose. I saw a side of you that I had never seen before. It was like this void that had been there your whole life had been filled in – by your own mother. You began to have goals in life, hopes and dreams, valuing yourself, paying attention to what you ate, working out, running marathons – it was wonderful to see. A couple of times you went back to drinking, but I knew that once you had gotten a taste of how it was to live a normal life, you would go back to it again – and you did.

I saw a smart, young man develop before my very eyes, and you saw yourself as a worthy human being. You enrolled at college and began to pursue a degree. You are living your dream, studying at a university overseas, committed to finishing your schooling and pursuing your career. I am so proud.

I want you to know, though, that I still hold my breath. For some reason, you seem to think that you can do all of this and still have a bottle of wine at night. It makes me afraid – afraid that you will lose everything you have fought for. It does not take away the pride I have for you, but it does make me hold my breath a little. In my experience working on a rehab unit, I have never seen an addict be able to use in moderation, they always slide back into their old ways. But for now, I am watching you work toward your goals, maintain your grades in college and continue to find ways to better enhance your inner self. I am choosing to focus on that, and not on the fact that there is always that chance that you will slip back into your old ways.

Please know, little brother, that no matter what, I always have my arms around you; that no matter where we both go in life, or how far away we are from each other, my arms are always holding you, singing lullabies to the little boy inside you, and making you feel safe. I love you for everything that you are, I am proud of your accomplishments, and I believe in you.

Your big sister is still praying for you and will never lose hope in you.

A young woman's haunting words to her sister whom she lost to anorexia.

I Believe In You

I do not believe in God.
I struggle with scriptures, sermons and most forms of
  organised religion.
Heaven and Hell are filed away in my mind, along
  with mermaids and dragons and a whole host of other
  childhood acquaintances.
And so how is it that I believe in you?

And I believe in you, not as a passing thought or a fleeting
  moment of reminiscence.
And you are more than a ghost of things past; things that
  were, but are no more.
I believe in you as a presence, an entity, a being. I believe
  in you as you.

But why do I believe in your existence, when it was so
  difficult to imagine your survival in this world, once the
  certainty of your death had plundered our lives?
You were there one day, but gone the next.
Stolen from us as we slept. The passing night leaving
  only the embers of your life; the life you were born to
  live, but yet somehow destined to destroy.
And we watched you, watching that. A tortured hallow,

forced to hold the devil's hand as he waltzed you to
tunes that you could never even have conceived of.

But now, on those rare occasions when we meet in
    dreams, or the shadow of your soul blows through me,
    it is you I meet.
You, my sister, in all your glory. And how your laughter
    bellows and your spirit shines. You fill every ounce of
    me with friendship, love and you.

And that is what I take from those moments.
That you are you once again, and that I have found you.

A man apologises to his friends and family for the hurt his addiction has caused them.

Thank You

I am writing this letter of appreciation and gratitude to everyone who has helped me along the way to my recovery.

I have learned a great deal of things about my addiction, myself, and other people over the last while. I've come to accept that I will be an addict for the rest of my life and that's been very hard for me to do.

I can choose to use drugs and suffer the consequences of my actions or choose to live, hopefully, a long drug-free life.

I'm beginning to accept and respect myself and other people for who and what they are rather than what I want them to be.

Not so long ago my life was in tatters. Well, to a great degree it still is. I owe a lot of money and have lost my wife and the life I once knew. But I have my health and I'm hopeful that I can get back to work and salvage some happiness in my life again. I would love to be able to fulfil some of the dreams I once had.

I hurt a lot of people along the way and I don't know if I will ever be fully forgiven by everyone for that. I am truly sorry if I hurt you. I never meant to hurt anyone – in a selfish way I thought I was only hurting myself.

I am so thankful and grateful to the people who have let me back in their lives, especially my mam and my brothers and sisters. Without you I would not be here today.

K

A sister writes to her deceased brother about how she misses him, and her feelings around his addiction.

Dear Joe

I'm unsure just when the problems began. I suppose I did have my suspicions that things weren't right when you started borrowing the money from me. You should have been managing better, you had a really great job. But then you'd reassure me, it was just a temporary problem, and that you were due a cheque to clear, or some other excuse like that.

You had excuses for everything – the eventual lost job, your broken relationship and even when you got evicted.

But you couldn't disguise the gaunt look on your face, the weight loss and the eventual health problems.

By the time we realised just how bad your drink problem was, you were very deep into your addiction – it had a firm grip on you.

We all tried to talk to you, to reason with you, to beg you, but nothing worked. You were the topic of discussion in many phone calls amongst the family. We were hard on you at times but we loved you and just wanted to help you – we just didn't know how. In the end, all we asked was for you to call us every now and then, to let us know that you were alive.

Thank God that Mam and Dad were not around to

see your eventual demise on the streets. The hardest part was seeing this highly intelligent man in such a dirty and psychotic state. Where did this angry and abusive man come from?

You were in my prayers every night. I'd ask God to give you the strength to get better, to protect you and to end the suffering.

At times I felt that the rest of the family had abandoned you – they were getting on with their lives; it was like you didn't exist anymore.

I suppose I always knew how it would eventually end. But nothing could have prepared me for that day. Before they even said the words, I knew that you were gone. I knew that you were dead. My worst nightmare: I had failed you.

So now you're gone but the guilt, the pain, the hurt, the shame, and the heartbreak remain.

Your sister

A woman addresses her anorexia in a letter, describing how her recovery has helped her to find out who she is and to love that person.

Dear Anorexia

I have come a long way since the first day we met. I don't need you nearly as much as I did before, and that's a good thing. For so long I have hated you, and now the hate has lessened. I think I am beginning to understand you and why I needed you so much.

I also feel that we are both trying to trust each other and, believe me, I know how difficult that is. That 'trust' word does not come easily to me, or, should I say, it didn't come easily to me. I am beginning to see that you *can* trust people in this world, and have relationships where people don't abandon you, or leave you.

I don't want you to be a part of my life anymore, but I don't know if that is possible. I will have to deal with that. I realise that for the past 20 years, I really needed you.

You never left me; you made me feel safe; I could always count on you. You gave me power and control when I needed it, but you did this in a very destructive and harmful way. That's where the anger comes in and why I hated you so much.

The arguments we would have in my head nearly killed me. I could no longer stand them, which is why I got help! You made me do things that were *disgusting*. Like abuse laxatives, lose a lot of weight, lie to everyone (including myself), be secretive, isolate myself from everyone. The ones who were hurt the most by this isolation were my kids – they didn't have a mother for a long time.

I was always angry and hungry. You made me starve myself. You made me have medical conditions from the eating disorder (some I still have). I felt worthless, had no self-esteem, and my recovery has been one of the hardest things in my life to go through. I nearly lost everything because of you, including my life! How could you do this to someone? Me, or *anyone* for that matter.

You take lives away and don't even care, because you are still out there grabbing on to someone else. You should be ashamed of yourself – it shouldn't be us feeling guilt and shame. I was 16 when you came into my life, you had no right to! I was just a kid! Now, for the past 20 years of my life, I have done nothing but live with you, fight with you, and not even know who I am.

You have taken 20 years of my life, and I had no choice about it. Now, for the past four years, I have been trying to get rid of you, so you can't hurt me anymore (I have had enough hurt in my lifetime). I would like to do this in a positive way, not a destructive way, like you did. I can't say I forgive you completely, but I am trying to understand you and why I still need you at times.

I am *not* a bad person (like you said I was), and if you would only let yourself see that, as all the wonderful people I have met through my recovery process have done. They really do care about *me*, not what I look like or how much I weigh. It's *me* they care about. The inside stuff. And do you know what a wonderful feeling that is, to have someone care about me, for me? I don't have to be *thin* to be *loved*! I don't need your protection anymore, nor do I have to pretend to be someone else.

I know that during the time you have been around, I needed you to protect me, to let me feel safe and worthy of myself, but I don't need that from you anymore. I can protect myself (in a healthy way), and I am beginning to love myself and find out who I am.

A girl thanks her parents for their support, as she learns to cope with her eating disorder and value herself once again.

Dear Mam

I am writing this letter to say thank you. I am so grateful for everything you have done for me.

You know the hardest part of all this has been me admitting to myself that I have an eating disorder. I'm glad I'm getting help now. I want to recover, I want to be free. I don't want to be sick anymore. I wish these inner voices would just go away. They are my biggest enemy – they don't want me to stop and they can be very loud at times, but I'm learning new skills to deal with them now.

I know it's going to take a lot of work and time to fully reach my recovery. As my counsellor said, I did not develop this overnight, so I'm sure not going to beat it overnight either.

I realise that I cannot do this alone and I am so grateful that you and Dad are there for me. I'm sorry for the hurt and worry I have caused.

I've been on a very scary journey but I'm ready to change. I'm finally dealing with the underlying issues, and learning to love and accept myself. I'm learning new, healthier ways of coping.

I'm looking forward to getting back to college and being with my friends again. I know there's a beautiful life out there for me. All I have to do is convince myself that I am worthy of it. But I'm starting to have faith and belief in myself, and it feels good.

Looking forward to your visit.

Love,
Your daughter

Awareness

'Step by step, let whatever happens happen.
Real change will come when it is brought about, not
by your ego, but by reality. Awareness releases
reality to change you.'

Anthony de Mello, from Awareness

Whether in addiction, or coping with someone you love in addiction, it can be hard to face certain home truths about the addictive situation. The reality is that when awareness comes to the fore, change follows. For as long as we wish to deny change, we can deny reality too.

Self-awareness requires honesty and courage – to get in touch with what we are thinking and feeling, and to face the truth about the addictive situation. Awareness is the first step to breaking the negative cycle we're in. It takes real courage to face addiction and get the help we need, and it comes from focussing our attention within, and becoming aware of both our power and our limitations. As we've touched upon, we have to accept that we are powerless over our addiction, or that of our loved ones. But through heightened self awareness – of our personalities, our emotions, how our pasts have shaped our present-day behaviour – we grow in awareness and we begin to come into contact with our power for change from within.

What do we need to do to gain self-awareness?

Self-awareness, in the simplest terms, is the discovery of who we really are. It enables us to discover our likes and dislikes, strengths and weaknesses; in essence, our own individuality.

Honesty leads to true self-awareness, and honesty requires courage. Dishonesty becomes easy when someone is trying to protect their addiction. The person in addiction will lie about how much and how often they have acted out in addiction. They will hide feelings and emotions, or become distant from relationships. Family members may lie to protect their loved one. Awareness and honesty are very closely linked, and are vital when it comes to stepping into the recovery process. According to Stedman Graham, author of *You Can Make It Happen*, self-awareness is a key to self-acceptance, which drives self-motivation and self-fulfilment. As he puts it: 'What you are aware of, you are in control of; what you are not aware of is in control of you.'

Awareness of a problem, be it addiction or living with the addiction of a loved one, can be very painful as it forces us to take steps to remedy the situation. It has often been said that when a person in addiction becomes aware of their problem it is the first step towards recovery. Awareness leads to acceptance and ultimately to positive change. For the person who has a loved one in addiction, the awareness of the problems caused by this is the first step towards solving the problem. This can mean that one learns to detach and enter into their own recovery.

Frances

Singer Mary Coughlan writes about her addiction and how she, and her family, found healing.

If you need to turn everything around in your life, then this letter is to you.

It may sound strange, but at this point in my life, I am glad about the way things have turned out. True, I've played havoc with myself and my family's lives; I have been in hospital, so near to death with tubes coming out of my heart – I have literally been brought to my knees by addiction. And sure, some really terrible things have happened as a result of my alcohol addiction, but believe it or not, I am thankful for all that has happened because I have learned so much about life. I know and understand myself so much better now.

I have five children, and, of course, I regret the trauma and loneliness my drinking caused them over the course of 15 years. When you are drinking, you block all this out – you just don't see it. It was not until I went into The Rutland Centre for six weeks, and became sober, that I was forced to look at their pain and accept the impact my drinking was having upon my family. It only needed to be a few sentences from each, it was enough, enough to make me stop, but, in all honesty, I only realised it at that point!

The healing process is a long one, and it takes a long time to trust yourself again, whatever about others trusting you. But I do trust myself now, so it's ok. It also takes a long time to forgive yourself. That's really hard. But I do now, for everything that's been – all of it. I'm not so hard on myself now. I understand that given my personal circumstances and the environment I grew up in, it was entirely natural to be unwell – anybody coming from a similar situation would be unwell too. My reaction was to drink. Not everyone behaves or reacts in the same way, but that's what I did.

When I went into The Rutland Centre, I began to receive counselling – my counsellor (who only much later became and is still my very dear friend) was literally my lifeline. It was at this point that I truly came to face my demons. I was able to trust my counsellor 100 per cent and tell my story without any judgement at all – only true compassion. It was through support and professional counselling that I was able to finally address the source of my pain and the reasons why I became addicted to alcohol and drugs. Through counselling, I learned to look at myself differently and accept myself. I had the space and time I needed, and experienced support to get me where I needed to go. I learned new coping mechanisms which I still use today.

From an early age (my teens), I was interested in and had read around the subject of family therapy and healing as a unit. My best friend, who is now a psychiatrist, gave me lots of reading material (even back then, I was trying to understand myself and my family, and find healing). A person usually doesn't get sick all by themselves, and so they rarely get better all by themselves – I am a true believer that we are a product of the environment we grow up in. Everyone has a role to play, and children take on roles in chaotic or unusual circumstances in their upbringing. To heal, the whole family needs to learn about addiction, to understand, to get better together, to forgive, to accept.

I still look after myself on a daily basis. I live in Wicklow and make sure I get out and walk in the hills every day. It's beautiful. I am blessed. I take time out for myself at least once a year and go on a holiday that is both therapeutic and good fun. And the people I love, they inspire me. I am a different person now than I was back then: I am sober and well, I look after myself, and I live life to the full. I live every minute to the full.

Mary

A mother of three writes to her counsellors about finally coming to terms with her son's drug addiction, without guilt.

Dear Counsellor

My son was into drugs and my home life revolved around his addiction. I tried everything. I tried to get him to go and see a counsellor or doctor, but he didn't keep any of the appointments. I was offered therapies that I took to help me cope with what we were all going through. I knew then it was up to him to make the appointments if he wanted to stop taking drugs. He had tried committing suicide. I was out of my mind. He has a son, my one and only grandson. He broke up with his partner. It was heartbreaking.

I have a daughter and son still living at home who, at the time, were trying to study for exams. It was difficult for them to cope and concentrate, it was impossible for them. There was constant worry and pressure on the whole family; we were always waiting for the next outburst of anger, usually when he needed more drugs. I knew in my heart that, I shouldn't allow this to happen at my home, as he was in his twenties, old enough to have his own space, which might enable him to be more of a responsible person. I decided that I would ask him to go. I worried myself sick, felt guilty and all the other emotions that a mother feels. I just needed somewhere or someone to talk to who understood what I was going through.

I was asked to go on an away week with my support group last year. At the time I was so grateful to get away from the worry of home life, and I was made to feel so welcome. Rathlin Island, where we went, is so beautiful and peaceful, so serene that I could quieten my mind and put things into perspective. On hearing similar words from the other people in the group, I knew I had done the right thing. I knew that while he was living at home, I was actually making matters worse. It was allowing him to have more freedom with his money to use it on drugs, when he should have been using it to find his own place.

He has since found a place sharing with a friend. He has bills to pay and a lot more responsibility. He still takes drugs but not on the scale that he was then. He knows I'm here if he wants help to deal with his addiction. He visits regularly and stays over when his son is here. My daughter and son both did well in their exams and I was able to carry on with my work. With the help of my support group, I got the courage to deal with and stand up to my son's addiction. I don't feel guilty anymore. Life is much happier for everyone.

Anonymous

*A woman writes a goodbye letter
to her addiction.*

Farewell, dear addiction. You were there for me when I needed you most. When my mother died you were my comfort. When I was scared you made me feel safe. When I was alone you were always there for me. You comforted me through pain and sorrow and you were always around to help me celebrate my victories. I never gave you credit for all the times you stayed with me when I was at the bottom of the heap. You gave me a voice and although it was not a voice heard by anyone but me, it was with me constantly, chattering away non-stop like white noise.

You gave me the ability to be invisible, a gift that served me well and probably saved my life. However, and there is a huge however, all these things you gave me came at a price. I was never allowed to grieve because I hid with you behind closed doors. I never developed courage because you told me that the substance I craved would take away all fear and protect me. I isolated myself and had no meaningful relationships because the wall between me and others (which you helped me build) was ten feet thick and made with stones of fear held together by mortar made from resentments, lies, shame and guilt.

You told me I was unworthy or that others weren't good enough, and most of the time I was unable to see a person's true self because I was kept enveloped in a fog. The fog you created for me to keep me safe, in the shadows, unseen. My pain and sorrow grew because I never worked through it. And every time I felt some hope you were there to whisper in my ear: 'You don't have to go there. Stay here with me, I will keep you safe. I am comfortable and I am your life.'

I listened to you, thinking you were my closest friend. And then one day I heard a different voice. A hand reached out to me. Gradually I stepped into the light. I sometimes saw a glimpse of you smirking as I fell back into your waiting arms time and time again. I heard you laughing as I told others about you. You thought I would never break free and sometimes I thought you were right. But there is something much stronger than you, and that is God. I saw the light and I heard someone's sweet voice say, 'You can have this – you can be free.'

All those years when I thought you were my friend you were scheming behind my back. Slowly, you robbed me of my dignity, joy and faith, and you did it with a smile and a lie. I always believed you until I saw the light, and with it the difference between the lie and the truth.

So here we are. It has taken a long time. You and I are looking for different things. You want me bound, desperate and alone, and I want release. I want to be free. I want to grieve, feel fear, grow courage, experience pain, hunger, happiness, love, disappointment, and joy. I thank you and I release you. Go to wherever addictions go when they are no longer needed or wanted, when they have finally been exposed to the light. It's okay to leave. I'm stronger now.

I can see through the fog. I have seen the truth, I've

experienced the light of God. We weren't made for each other anyway. I was meant to live and walk with a source greater than you. I was meant to be, to feel. I was meant to live unchained. Go attach yourself to another. You and I no longer exist together. I release you with love, but I do release you completely. But know this, I will be watching. If I see you deceiving others, I will share the light with them. I will expose you and your lies. So, you liar, cheat and thief: farewell, skedaddle, adios, arrivederci, ciao, auf wiedersehen, so long, goodbye, adieu, hit the road Jack and don't come back!

Anonymous

A woman writes to her dad about the lingering effects from childhood of his addiction on her life.

Dear Dad

When I was young, I felt that you loved me and that all your friends thought I was the cutest baby. We lived in England, and life was good for you and Mom with plenty of work and a good social life. You were both young when you had me and full of hope for the future.

We returned to Ireland when I was a toddler, and life became harder then. It was the sixties and we had a farm with no electricity or running water. For a while, I had an idyllic time with freedom to run around the fields and be in nature. When I went to school, I was a shy child and did as I was told.

Dad, you began to go away a lot to work, once for two years when I was five or six. I felt abandoned and was angry at you for leaving us. I did not understand that you had to go abroad to earn money for the family. Nobody talked to children about what was going on in those days, so I came to the conclusion that I must have done something wrong for you to leave me.

I first noticed your drinking being a problem when I was around seven years old. Mom would be angry at you when you came home from the pub, and once, you forgot that I was supposed to go to my friend's birthday party, and Mom was really angry at you for disappointing me.

We moved from a country to a town when I was ten and I hated it. Your drinking was getting worse. Money was tight and it felt like we were always walking on eggshells. We never spoke to each other about what was really going on, all living in our own separate little worlds. As a teenager, I disappeared into TV, food, sleep and romance novels to escape the tension in our home.

When I was around 15, Mom threatened to leave you, and the doctor told you that you would die if you continued drinking. That was my lowest point, as I was afraid we would all be split up and have to go to the poor house. You got sober for good in AA when I was 17, and that has been a great blessing for the whole family.

I moved away from home when I was 17 to work. Life was good – I had a good job and a great social life. It was mostly centred around pubs and discos. I was always worried that I might turn into an alcoholic so was careful, and didn't drink too much. I loved to dance. I seemed to be the one who looked after everyone, and made sure they got home safely, particularly the ones who drank a lot.

When I was 21, I fell in love for the first time. It was very intense and I was totally obsessed with him. He drank a lot and did drugs, and was very unpredictable. I thought I would change him, and that he would settle down with the help of my love. After a year, he went abroad and never told me he was going. I was devastated, and very hurt.

I fell in love again at 27, and at 33, I went to America

to live with my boyfriend, who I had been with for six years. His drinking was very bad at that time, and I was very concerned for him. I hoped that he would 'see the light', and stop drinking, and that we could get married and have a family.

After a few weeks, we were at a party one night, and I walked in on him making love to another woman. I fell apart at that stage and decided to end my life. The pain was unbearable. I rang my Mom in Ireland and she suggested I go to Al-Anon. I went to get help for him, but over time, learned to stay for me. That was the beginning of my healing.

Since then, Dad, I have learned to love and forgive you and Mom, and all the alcoholic men that were in my life. My relationship with you and Mom is good now, and I accept that you are human, and that you did the best you could at the time. I have learned to be gentle with myself and my humanity.

Today, I am on my own and sometimes I feel lonely, and sad that I never got married or had children. I feel sad that because of alcoholism, you never really knew me, or how to connect to your children, or to yourself.

Alcoholism has caused great damage in all our lives, but it has taught us to love, accept and care for each other too. Thank you for getting sober, and for being there for your family today.

I love you.

Anonymous

A woman talks about her own recovery as the mother of a daughter with an addiction.

A Letter to Alcohol

You are the snake in the grass that sidled up to my child, sensing her addictiveness. Did you leave her alone, give her a chance? No, you charmed her, deceived her into thinking you could help her feel better, be better. When she realised you were lying, it was too late – she had succumbed to your coaxing, convinced she could not live without you.

You knew the effect this would have on me and all the family. Watching my child distracted, defeated, desperate, disintegrating in front of my eyes has been hell. I fought to wrestle her from your grip – pouring you down the drain, talking, coaxing, persuading, threatening and pleading with her, telling her that you had no right to her life. It didn't work; your stronghold proved too much for both of us.

I despaired. I cried out in pain watching her suffering, her slide into hell. Worse, I watched you tear my other children apart, crying for their sister, trying to help her as I had already tried. When they admitted defeat, they turned on one another. You destroyed my whole family, not just my child! I looked for ways to end my life.

Thank God I found RISE and got the chance to recover before it was too late. The week I spent on

Rathlin Island was a turning point. I was with people concerned about me and my healing. They listened to my crying, acknowledged my pain, and wrapped me in a warm healing hug. They gently led me away from the bad place you had taken me to. They showed me a route back, and are helping me to stay on that route.

I call it recovery. It's a slow, but scenic, route back. Slow, because it is difficult to change my mindset and feelings. I must take it one day at a time. Some days I make good progress. Other days, the road is slow and hard – I can sense your evil presence, and I know I must talk to my friends in RISE.

Scenic, because I now appreciate the important things in my life – family, home, walking, sunlight, shared time with healthy friends. There is the ripple effect of healing in the house. My children are reconciling. I hope my addicted child will catch the healing too.

She was relieved when I told her I was going to get help for myself. I know that deep down she wants help to escape from your grasp. I am more accepting of her illness since I came back from Rathlin. I love her, and pray that she will succeed in escaping from your horror, Alcohol. May she find her RISE – Recovery In a Safe Environment.

Whatever happens, you will not drag me down into your hell ever again.

Anonymous

*A woman speaks of how she is living proof
that no addict is a lost cause.*

I spent many, many years addicted to alcohol. From when I took my first drink at the age of 17 until I sought help at 32, I can honestly say that I was completely at the mercy of alcohol. It controlled my life, and it came to the point that I could not function without it. I was always a 'blackout drinker' – I would start my night in one place, and when I would come to, I would be in a completely different place and have no recollection of how I got there.

Drink not only had an impact on my life, but its rippling effect meant it impacted those whom I loved the most. My marriage broke down because of alcohol, and my parents constantly worried about me. They became very frail. They never knew where I was or what I was doing, or whether I would return home unharmed. While in the midst of my addiction, I never thought of these people; the only thing I thought about was how I could get my next drink. Many times my mother sat on my bed, crying and begging me to please stop. She could not understand how I could want to drink, when I was lying in bed shaking uncontrollably and dry-retching. I could not see the pain I was inflicting on my family. In my mind at that time, another drink would stop the shakes and remove the sickness.

The vicious circle that alcoholism is, continued for

many years. I woke up many times lying outside, covered in bruises and cuts. I lost my dignity and self-respect; I also lost my job, but still I did not think I had a problem. In 2007 I became homeless and ended up in a psychiatric unit, due to the effects of alcohol. I had to be fed in the unit, because my shakes were so bad. Physically and mentally, I had hit my rock bottom. I stayed in this unit for over two months, and, while in there, I admitted that alcohol was a major problem in my life.

Although I didn't realise it then, I can now see that this was the first day my life would change for the better. When I was discharged from the unit, I left feeling full of fear, afraid of going out and possibly returning to drink. I immediately sought help and began to follow a 12-step programme. The first six months of recovery were extremely difficult. My disease kept trying to tell me I could be a successful social drinker, that thankfully I didn't succumb to these thoughts. I am now, one day at a time, sober for over three years.

To anyone who has an addiction, there is help out there. I personally believe that no addict is a lost cause. It is a disease, but, with a lot of determination and willpower, it can be controlled on a daily basis. I am proof of that. Once, I could not go one day without drinking to the point of a blackout. Now, my life is fantastic. I am free today to do anything I wish. I always say that there are so many things I can do, but one thing that I can never do is take a drink. Seek help and hang in there, and eventually the clouds will be lifted and the sun will shine in your life.

A daughter remembers the uncertainty of her childhood, waiting for her alcoholic father to come home.

I suppose, because you are just a child, you don't know how other families operate and so you don't know what you are missing. You do know that you are always worried and unhappy and waiting for the next thing to happen: will he come home? If he does, will he be drunk? If he's drunk, will he be a happy one, or a sad one, or an angry one?

Whatever kind of man he was each evening, we were all walking on eggshells around him, afraid to upset or agitate him, even for a second, in case you'd be the one to start the abuse or the crying or the violence.

My mother was always afraid of what would happen. He wouldn't answer his phone and so she would ask us to ring him. Sometimes, I realise now, he wouldn't answer even when he was sober, because he liked it when we worried, and then he could turn up, full of the joys, as if to prove that she was a nag and that there was nothing to worry about.

He was a great man for socialising and for organising parties in the house. There would be a day and a half of good humour and preparation, but we all knew that it would end up the same whether it was my birthday, Christmas, a First Communion or just a summer barbeque. He would be drunk and we would all be tip-toeing around trying to avoid him, hoping he would just go to bed and go to sleep.

The worst was when he would get drunk and then go out again. Then we knew my mother would not sleep and we would all be straining to hear the sound of the car and the key in the door.

On the morning after my ninth birthday, I came downstairs to find him vomiting into a bucket on the floor of the front room and I heard my mother on the phone, telling his work that he had a stomach bug. I went into school and all the girls said it had been a great birthday party and what great craic my father was. I smiled and said thanks for coming, but I had a knot in my stomach, wondering what the story would be when I got home.

It was always the same, and all that has an effect on you. My mother and my brother and I eventually ran away from him and there was a lot of trouble, but everyone thought that once we weren't living with him, everything was okay.

It took a long time for me to find The RISE Foundation and to talk about it all. It was a great relief to find someone to understand and to tell me that it was okay to feel angry and hurt by it all. Just that changed how I felt and released a lot of emotions. I am much better for that and can let go of a lot of the pain.

A woman explains how counselling and support helped her come to terms with her husband's addiction.

I was really at the end of my tether when I finally sought help.

This was after decades of being emotionally battered by alcoholism in my life, first in my own family, then in my husband's family and then in my husband himself.

It is easier to be an addict than in a family with alcoholism, I think. At least the addict escapes into the drink or the drug or the gambling or whatever, but the family just sits and waits for the next crisis.

I spent nearly 20 years trying to fix everything and to control a drinker who just got worse and worse, as a drunk and as a person, over that time.

Because we are from Ireland, everyone thinks they know what alcoholism is and what it does, but unless you are in it, you don't know how it eats up your soul and destroys all the relationships and love in a family.

I felt I would never forgive my husband for what he did to the children and to me, but I was so dependent on everyone being dependent on me, that it was really me who needed the help.

It took me time to feel that everything wasn't my fault and that I could not control him no matter how I tried. As soon as I came back from a week with RISE on Rathlin Island, my children and friends noticed the change in me. They said I even looked different. That was because I was not carrying that burden of guilt around with me and, instead of looking ahead in despair, I began to feel I could look after myself, that I was allowed to do that and the alcoholic had to look after himself too.

I will never forget what RISE did for me. That week in Rathlin salvaged my life for me and I can't believe the difference it has made.

*An alcoholic-in-recovery recognises a
turning point in her relationship
with her daughter.*

My daughter rang me this morning. She was in the city centre on a field trip for her college course and suddenly felt unwell. Without hesitation, I grabbed my coat and bag and told her I was on the way. Not long after, we were having coffee and all was well. Nothing unusual there – it's what any parent would do – but a year ago she would not have phoned me, or trusted me to help her, because my name is Barbara and I am an alcoholic.

A year ago, most probably I would have been drinking, or sick from yet another feeble attempt at stopping. My mind, body, and soul were capable of helping neither my daughter nor myself. Alcohol was my family, my friend, my reason to get up in the morning, my life. The tears, the arguments, the pleading from my family for me to stop had no effect. They didn't understand that, to me, drink was my lifeline, and I just wanted to be left alone.

Thankfully, they never gave up on me, even when I had given up on myself. They supported me when I started attending counselling with Frances, and together we fight, and today we won again. They are the first ones I tell if I have the urge to drink, and they never tire of my asking for help. I can never turn back the clock and erase the hurt and worry I caused them, but I hope my being sober shows them that they are m*y family, my friends, my reason to get up in the morning* – m*y life.*

To *my* family, my guardian angels, thank you for helping me to find *my* soul.

*A mum and sisters write to their son and brother
who passed away after a drug overdose.*

Dear Paulie

You are missed so much. Our hearts are broken since you died from an accidental overdose less than a year ago. You struggled so hard in recovery. I just wish there were more services for young men like you, somewhere to be safe and supported. I wish with all my heart that things were different, and addiction did not get its horrible claws into you. You are loved so much. We miss your smile and humour and your quirky ways, we just miss having you with us. When you were in active addiction it was a nightmare, but that nightmare has been eclipsed by your death. Every day is an even bigger struggle now for all of us left behind.

*All our love,
Mum and your sisters xxxx*

A survivor of the impact of addiction asserts her identity.

I'm Me

I'm strong
I'm fearless
I'm considerate
I'm tough-skinned
I'm self-sufficient
I'm independent
I'm not needy
I'm reliable
I'm hard
I'm soft
I'm understanding
I'm sensible
I'm kind
I'm a good friend
I'm tough
I'm a carer
I'm alive
I'm a survivor
I'm Not a Victim
I'm ok
I'm me.

We Laughed, We Cried . . .

After one of the many suicide threats and being locked out of the house again, we were trying to figure out if the still, seemingly 'lifeless' body we could see through the window was alive or dead.

'Oh, Jesus, he's dead. Oh my God, kick the door in. Ring the police.'

'Stop, stop will ye, he's not dead.'

'How do you know?'

'Well, look, there's a full glass of wine on the floor at his feet – he'd never leave that behind!'

And, true to form, the hand leaned slowly down and picked it up.

'Call the police.'

'Why?'

'Cause I'm going to kick the door down and f**king kill him!'

Acceptance

'Anything in life that we don't accept will simply make
trouble for us until we make peace with it.'

Shakti Gawain

Acceptance is a key factor when it comes to recovery from addiction.

Eckhart Tolle, author of *The Power of Now*, defines acceptance as a 'this is it' response to anything occurring in any moment of life. In any given moment, strength, peace and serenity are available when one stops struggling to resist or hanging on tightly to what is so.

Acceptance does not mean resignation to the sorry and miserable way things may seem in a given moment. It doesn't mean accepting or tolerating any sort of abuse. It means that, in the now, we acknowledge and accept our circumstances, including ourselves and the people in our lives, as we and they are. It is with acceptance that we are able to receive the power to change the things we can.

For example, the person in addiction cannot stop their drinking, drugging, gambling etc. until they accept their powerlessness over whatever addiction they may have. It is the same for the family member – it is not until they too accept their powerlessness over their loved one in addiction that true freedom evolves.

As the Serenity Prayer tells us, it is necessary that we learn 'to accept the things we cannot change, and the courage to change the things we can'. Once we have accepted that we are powerless over addiction, then we can start the recovery process. As we come out of the isolation of addiction by asking for help and not resisting change, we can allow ourselves to move towards a new way of living. For the person in addiction, acceptance may be difficult; denial and underestimation of their addiction can come into play. Therefore, attending a support group like AA, going to a treatment centre (outpatient or residential), or visiting an addiction counsellor can be vital.

If you are a family member or concerned person, you may struggle with acceptance also. The anxiety that you may feel is often compounded by the belief that you somehow caused or contributed to your loved one's addiction, or that you could have done something to prevent it. You don't want to believe what is happening to them.

Some very normal personalised beliefs will come into play for you. For example:

'If I were a better mother/father/wife/husband/son/ daughter, you would love me enough to stop drinking/ using/acting out.'

'As a parent, I must have done something wrong to make you feel so bad that you have to take drink, drugs or act out in an addictive way.'

'I need to work harder to make sure you love me, and then you'll stop, and everything will be okay.'

Feelings of fear, shame, and confusion over a loved one's addiction can cause deep anxiety, sleepless nights, and even physical illness. The stress of living in a chronic state of chaos and being on edge all the time eventually takes its toll. Acceptance is the key to making a major life change for you. Like your loved one in addiction, it is important to tap into the support that is out there for family members. Learning to accept that you're powerless over the addictive situation, as well as over the person who has the problem, is vital. You are not responsible for the drinking, drug-taking, gambling, or behaviour of your loved one in addiction; you are only responsible for your own attitudes and behaviour.

Acceptance is the ultimate paradox: we cannot change who we are until we accept ourselves the way we are.

Frances

Paddy Creedon expresses how much he values being a part of the human race and how happy he is to be liberated from daily life as an alcoholic.

Recovery – The Preferred Option for People like me

Last October, I arrived at that magical milestone of my sixtieth birthday, sharing the date of 16 October with such literary icons as Oscar Wilde and Paul Durkin. Reaching and surpassing significant milestone dates for an alcoholic in recovery, which I have been now for over half my lifetime, gives me an ideal opportunity to reflect on a lifetime's journey – the ups, the downs, the challenges, the achievements, the great days, the good days, and the not so good days.

Normality, for an alcoholic in recovery like me . . . being and acting normally is probably my greatest lifetime achievement. The novelty of being part of the human race, with all its shortcomings, is still a daily reprieve from being an active and, what my medical advisor described me at the time as, chronic alcoholic. This chaotic lifestyle started with a glass of beer in a Dublin hotel in 1970 and ended seven years later with my decision to opt for a life of acceptance of my addiction to booze and to enter into a lifetime of Recovery, a day at a time.

Like any active alcoholic/addict, I had left behind a

wreckage of vast proportions, with family, friends and others affected by my totally unacceptable behaviour, unpredictabilities, and poor judgements. Understandably, they had given up on me many times. Today, life is so different: I stopped drinking, and, more importantly, I learned how to stay stopped. I have regained the trust of those most affected, and continue working on a daily programme for a lifetime of Recovery. You see, there is no finishing line or graduation ceremonies for people in recovery, other than a daily reprieve from the physical and mental obsessions that make up the insane behaviours of addiction.

Life presents a host of challenges, from minor to major, on an ongoing basis, and to be able to put one's complete trust in a way of living that is fundamentally spiritual in its essence, provides me with the daily framework to get on with my life as a sober alcoholic living a fulfilling life in recovery. This way of life brings me into contact with many wonderful people, and, more often than not, like-minded people who are determined to promote alternative ways of living for people and families that are affected by addictions. One such practical visionary is Frances Black, with her determination, through her RISE Foundation, to bring a lifelong solution to families who have been affected by the addictions of drink and drugs, now operating at epidemic proportions across Ireland. She needs and deserves our support, as, together, we have to enthusiastically adopt the greatest 'psycho-social challenge' in Ireland today: let's promote the concept of Addiction as the disease of Acceptance and no longer the disease of Denial, and in so doing remove forever all the negative stigmas that are associated with addiction in our communities – local and national.

One of the many benefits of my own personal and never-ending road to recovery is that some people spotted in me a 'creative streak' that was waiting to be developed. I am now an active member of the Irish Writers' Centre and working towards publishing some work in the not too distant future. Here's a short piece.

In Recovery

In slow rhythm,
she applies warm oil to her hands,
her healing skills unfold, as she moves
finger tip after finger tip,
paw-like across my scalp.

She touches my troubled racing mind,
running well ahead of itself as usual,
pressure point landing on pressure point,
she unravels, dismantles each mental roadblock,
freeing me from myself, everybody and everything.

With each new endorphin
running wild inside me now,
like a fuel-line flowing free
with my innermost thoughts,
love stories unfold, get shared.

Then by way of quiet conversation
she introduces me to myself,
Lowering her head, she whispers
"It's better for you, easier for me
if you don't talk so much."

A wife and mum writes to her husband
of how she has finally come to terms
with his addiction.

Dear Husband

This is the second letter I have written to you in the last couple of months and I fear that I will be putting the next one I write in your coffin with you. And the crazy part is that you seem oblivious to it all. But do you know something? I can honestly say that I have come to terms with this. I have come to realise that I can do nothing about this. This has taken me a while but I'm getting there. I do feel sad as it could all have been prevented if you had only made different choices and accepted the help offered to you. But I have accepted now that these choices were yours to make, not mine, and I was completely powerless over this.

The difference now is that, instead of our kids watching two sick parents grow older, I have done something to aid my recovery, as I can see now that your addiction to alcohol was making me sick too. I was turning into an angry, resentful, sad human being. I could see the kids picking up on my moods, and it was me they argued with because they had come to realise over the years that it was pointless having a go at you – you were always too drunk to care.

Anyway, while I can see you getting sicker, I can

feel myself getting stronger and better, and I honestly believe that if I hadn't found outside support, I would now be in a much darker place. Through seeking help, I have participated in both one-on-one counselling and the Family Group programme, and I really think that without them I would now be in a psychiatric hospital, or worse – in Mountjoy Prison. At RISE, I have never once felt like I was being judged, no matter what came out of my mouth, and, my God, some mad stuff has been said by me. No one told me that if I did this, you would get sober and better, and we would all live happily ever after. But, through group therapy, I was shown ways in which I could help my own recovery, and which, in turn, would help my children. There, I also learned to understand addiction and this has helped me to have a small bit of compassion for you.

There are still times when I feel angry with you, but, unlike before, I can now let it go. I am feeling much more positive about the future, but I miss that time when you and I were the best of friends. It used to be me and you against the world.

When I look at you now I feel so sorry for you. And even now I still wish for a miracle to happen. You look so alone, and still you think you don't need anyone else. It must be so sad to think like that. I wish you had sought some kind of programme to get yourself better, where you would have found like-minded people who wouldn't have judged you, but would have understood and supported you on your journey. Still, I can accept now that maybe you didn't want to get sober or were too afraid to.

When I think of how we were when we first met, fell in love, began our family. They were happy times. You always had my best interests at heart – a true gent from when we first dated, walking me all the way home if we missed the last bus, even if it got you in trouble with your dad. And later, when the kids came along, how you loved them and looked after us all!

I know I have lost the husband I once had and my kids have lost their father. I have lost a man who would have one time walked on hot coals if I had asked him. A man who once loved his wife with all his heart. I miss having you in the bed. I miss not having long conversations with you. I miss not being able to tell you about my day and share my worries and concerns with you. I miss not talking about our kids with you. I miss the joking and fun we used to have. It's still so hard to understand where that man went, and how it all came to this.

I really am so glad I found my counsellors and friends at the group as they have helped me come to terms with so much over the last few months, and I thank them from the bottom of my heart for their support and help. It is great that there is now somewhere for families to seek help and feel less alone at times of crisis, RISE really has been my saviour.

Going to sign off now, and I really hope you can find some kind of peace. Although I do say some horrible things about you, I know I really don't mean them.

Your Wife

Poem describing the childhood fear of night-time in the home of an alcoholic parent.

Tears and Fears

I am going to bed full of fear
under blankets with my tears
for Dad's gone out again for beers.
So I wait for footsteps on the stairs,
the front door opens with a bang,
he is back, I wait for the clang,
of empty cans dropped in the hall
or maybe thrown against the wall.
My mam's in bed, I hear her pacing
to and fro, her heart is racing
waiting for a drunken lout.
He comes upstairs,
I hear the shout,
'Where are you bitch?' I hear him say,
'Where is the bottle I hid away?'
My mam goes down and brings it up
I hear him shouting, 'Have a cup.'
It goes on like this day by day,
abuse to Mam in many ways.
Mental, physical, no one knows
but now Mam has said, 'Time to go'
so with the help of a foundation,
we're heading for the railway station

to our new home where we will live
with no more abuse or tears to shed.
We are happy now with good people,
I sleep at night, my mam's not weeping.
So if you are living with a drunken blight
there are people out there
who can bring you into the light.

*A mother's words to her daughter who is
in recovery from an eating disorder.*

Darling

The little curly-haired girl in the pink and white daisy
 dress sitting on the wall swinging her legs.
The angel Gabriel at the Nativity with halo
 half-slanted.
Then Halloween, the fairy witch in the wellies.
It was raining.
Innocence, Happiness, Calm.

Then came the teenage years.
The images bombarding in, at first ignored.
But they gained momentum like a predatory animal.

First went the treats. That was ok. Healthy eating.
Then the carbs in total.

It was May, school was out.
Off with friends. Eating lunch out, Mum.
There was no lunch.

 The clothes grew bigger. The hair grew thinner, fell
 out.
It was the night before France. You told us.
We were lucky. For us, it wasn't too late. They said.

Still the shock, the despair.
Therein followed the doctors, the long drives to get her
  help.

You were brave. You worked hard to fight it.
For us began the continual watching, wondering,
  listening at doors.
The despair watching you bake and eating none of it.
The early morning making of the smoothies while you
  slept. What goodness can we get in today?
For us, it took its toll. Sadness enveloped us like a
shroud. Our spirit crushed.

Then, like a phoenix out of the ashes, came The RISE.
We learned to set boundaries. We listened to others
  who were like us.
Their loved ones in addiction. We weren't alone. There
  was hope. We lived for the peace on Friday nights.

It's two years on now. You are doing so well. We are so
  proud.
We thank God for your redemption.
For us, we thank RISE for leading us through the
  darkness of the tunnel into the light

Mum

Words from a son-in-recovery about his mum, and the suffering that all mothers go through when their children are in pain.

Mothers are your silent friend
With you in the beginning through to the end
Through all your struggles when your heart breaks and
  bends
She is the one there to heal and mend.

Sometimes we forget that our mothers have feelings too
Sometimes we forget what they've been through
Just hold and love her as she would you.

Mothers often take on so much blame
Just to remove our own shame.

Never forget that they may have been in dark places
Yet all they desire is the smiles on our faces.

A mum writes to her son in addiction.

Dear Son

I was enchanted by you from the day you were born. You were our youngest, and loved and welcomed by your sister and brother. You were so cute with your curls and gorgeous brown eyes, an easy baby who had lots of attention from us all, especially your nana who was smitten from day one. She was fascinated by how quick you were to learn and by your incessant questions. You wanted to know the whys and hows of everything, and kept asking until you were satisfied that you understood.

You expected fairness most of all, and it was a challenge sometimes to explain why some things and some people weren't fair. You could never accept 'because they say so' or 'it just is', and I found it difficult myself to understand some of the things that happened too. On your first day of school, I watched with other parents through the school fence as you played in the yard, missing my baby and hoping you would be ok. I watched you approach a teacher in the playground and asked you afterwards what you had been saying. You had been running around and the teacher told a few of you to take it easy and not to run. The others stopped but you approached the teacher and explained that he was not your teacher – your teacher was in the classroom – so he was not to tell you what to do. I was shocked and did my best to explain that any teacher had the right to correct a pupil under their care. It was a sign of things to come. If you understood what was expected of you, you thrived and were at the top of the class. If there was conflict, it was challenged by you at length. I remember telling you that you had a right to think what you liked, but to keep it to yourself when it was appropriate.

There was very little to worry about in junior school as you were so quick to learn and loved being competitive. In secondary school you started to have more conflict. Because you had never got into the habit of studying – you didn't need to – you were finding it harder to be at the top of everything, and you were unhappy with yourself. I think that's when the trouble started. My lovely, bright, caring son was leaving us and we had no idea what was happening.

In hindsight, I should have suspected drugs. I was ignorant then. I thought someone on drugs would have glazed eyes and maybe sleep a lot. I didn't know a young teen who was becoming aggressive and distancing himself from us had a much more serious problem than going through the usual difficult teens. It was gradual but progressive. No more happy holidays, no more laughs as a family, no more bantering and sharing your news with us.

We got sick too, and lived in fear of what would happen next. There were rows, late nights out looking for you, the tension palpable when you arrived home. Later, there was the expulsion from school, the fights outside the house, the police calls to come to the station, and a broken family who had no idea we were enabling you to get sicker.

Paying off your debts, allowing totally unacceptable behaviour, being afraid to challenge you and pulling away from you emotionally. If someone asked me how I was, I started to explain what was currently happening with you. I lived from one drama to the next, and didn't give enough attention to your brother and sister. I stopped looking after myself and became the victim and the martyr. I became addicted to you. I was obsessed with your every move: checking up on you, trying to find out where you were, who you were with . . . I thought my children were an extension of myself, and that I was as responsible as you for your behaviour. You told us we were boring and you didn't want to end up like us, sitting there worrying, when your friends' parents went out drinking and having fun and didn't nag their kids.

You went to treatment centres and we supported you. But instead of getting better, you kept getting worse and eventually my fears were realised: you were sent to prison. We were a quiet, law-abiding family and no one we knew had been to court, let alone prison, so it was like a living nightmare. I think I detached from my emotions and went through the motions instead.

It was the turning point for me though. The situation was taken out of my hands and I was powerless. I started to read Al-Anon literature and found meetings and began to face myself. That decision was the beginning of a new life for me. It helped me to recognise when you were getting sick again, and this time I wanted to help you in the only way that works for all of us affected by addiction. I needed to get support for me; to find someone who understood; to get information about addiction from the professionals, and to have a safe place to share what was happening in my life. Addiction is a family disease and it is progressive.

When I got the proper support I needed for myself, it was the best thing I ever did. I am so much more aware now. I know I cannot cure you; I know I was never meant to play God with your life; I know I have to let you make your mistakes; I know I can make my own, and once I accept the consequences of my decisions and actions, I will learn and grow as a human, and maybe find my purpose in life. I know that it's okay to feel angry, upset and bereft, but also that I have a right to feel happy, loved and safe. I know if I take care of me and my business, and lead the best life I can, I will be doing the best for me and the best I can do for you too.

I love you with all my heart. I pray for you every day and I hope you find peace in your heart again.

Mum xx

*A woman writes of how the addictions
of her husband and now her son have
impacted on her life.*

When I first married my husband, I was blissfully happy, full of hopes and dreams. By our second wedding anniversary, he was a patient on an alcohol-treatment programme. During the first two years of our marriage, my dreams had been shattered and replaced by broken promises, my hopes and expectations replaced by despair and loneliness. I had never experienced such loneliness.

I was struggling to survive. My confidence was shattered and my self-esteem was at an all time low. I had lost my identity as a person. The support sessions at the treatment centre brought me both clarity and a sense of security. Driving through the gates to attend various meetings and a support group on Tuesday afternoons, I felt I'd arrived at my sanctuary. It was there I realised that I was not alone. The confused feelings I had were okay.

For the first time in two years I could identify with other people. With tremendous help and support from our counsellor there, I slowly began to emerge from the fog, and started to gain perspective on my life. I learned many valuable insights into myself and the nature of addiction, none more so than the realisation that the only person whose behaviour I could control was my own.

I left my husband ten years into our marriage with my one-year-old son. Though he had stopped drinking by then, the mental and physical abuse along with his proven infidelity had become too much to bear.

Having sought the protection of the courts through a series of Protection and Barring Orders, I found the courage to leave my home and escape from my abusive marriage. In the pursuit of his irresponsible, selfish lifestyle my husband had no qualms about doing whatever he believed was necessary to achieve his chosen way of life, even if it meant sacrificing our marriage and his relationship with our son.

As I write this piece, I am again dealing with addiction. My son is currently attending an addiction counsellor. I feel a great sense of loss as I feel that I have lost my child to addiction despite my best efforts. Familiar feelings have been brought to the surface once more and I struggle some days to deal with this burden again. I thought I had put all this behind me, I hope with help and support to get through this again.

Anonymous

An excerpt from 'Ride On' by Jimmy MacCarthy

The Contender
Jimmy MacCarthy

When I was young, and I was in my day
Sure I'd steal what woman's heart there was away
And I'd sing into the dawning
Song ablaze into the morning
Long before I was the man you see today
I was born beneath a star that promised all
I could have lived my life between Cork, Cobh and Youghal
But the wheel of fortune took me
From the highest point, she shook me
By the bottle live, by the bottle I shall fall

Chorus *There in the mirror on the wall*
I see the dream is fading
From the contender to the brawl
The ring, the rose, the matador raving

And when I die, I'll die a drunk down on the street
He will count me out to ten in clear defeat
Wrap the Starry Plough around me
Let the piper's air resound me
And there I'll rest until the Lord of Love I'll meet

Chorus *There in the mirror on the wall*
I see the dream is fading
From the contender to the brawl

The ring, the rose, the matador raving
Wrap the Starry Plough around me,
Let the piper's air resound me
And there I'll rest until the Lord of Love I'll meet

'The Contender' is a song about a man who had everything and blew it. Britain had never seen anything like Jack Doyle. In 1933, he drew 90,000 fans to the White City to watch him box. He was earning £600 a week on stage as a singer, and all of this at the age of nineteen. Born into a poor family in Cobh in County Cork in 1913, it was Jack Doyle's dream to fight like Jack Dempsey and to sing like John McCormack.

His good looks, charm and athletic figure brought him to Hollywood, where this fine-featured, six-foot-five Adonis socialised with such greats as Clark Gable and Errol Flynn. He had an affair with the motor-industry heiress Delphine Dodge. The singing playboy's motto was 'a generous man never went to hell' and, by the time he was thirty, he was well on his way to squandering his three-quarters-of-a-million-pound fortune.

Later he fell in love with the Mexican singer and movie star, Movita. He married her and they returned to Britain and Ireland where their touring show reaped huge financial rewards. The couple achieved a celebrity status comparable to Burton and Taylor, arguably more attractive but with equal fire in their relationship. But Jack's drinking, carousing and sexual exploits destroyed the marriage. Movita fled to America and Doyle ended up singing for his supper in the bars of London and Dublin, where he spent much of his time in a brothel in the red-light district run by the legendary Madam Dolly Fawcett, who held the fallen idol in great and tender esteem. Movita later married Marlon Brando.

Doyle never really got over the love of his life. He missed Movita desperately as he sank, literally, to gutter level. But throughout his bad times, he maintained an incredible spirit and dignity as he moved through the netherworlds of Dublin and London, where he died penniless on the streets in 1978. He was brought back in triumphant fashion to his native Cobh where he was buried with great style and celebration.

I first heard something of the Jack Doyle story from my father, who got drunk with the legendary hell-raiser when Jack and 'Iron Man' Butty Sugrue, on their way to a demonstration bout at Puck Fair in Killorglan, dropped into the Terence Hotel bar in Macroom, which belonged to my grandmother Hannah MacCarthy. She had bought the premises when it was called The Victoria but changed the name to The Terence in memory of the hunger striker Terence MacSweeney.

This was my parents' first home after they married and it was here I was born on 28 January 1953. Some years later, my father discovered Alcoholics Anonymous and adhered to its philosophy for the rest of his life, bar the occasional lost weekend. I returned home to my parents' house at the age of thirty and, with my father's incredible support, I surrendered to the same programme – to hand my life over to God as I understood him to be, and, one day at a time, not to take that first drink. I have been sober now for 19 years and, though still very far from perfect, I feel I owe my blessed life to this programme. I wonder if Jack Doyle had found his way into any of the countless AA rooms all over the world would his story have been a different one. It was with this recognition of a fellow alcoholic that I wrote 'The Contender' and 'That Face'.

'That Face' is a collection of lyric scraps that were all written in a state of hangover (at which I excelled) and conveniently fell together to make this piece.

That Face
Jimmy MacCarthy

Spirit and bright one
Have you left me for dead?
Once light burned in these eyes
Now they're pale and bled
I see morning with no mystery
And the darkness holds only dread for me
And so it goes when you travel by bottle
Ride the wall of death
Blind on full throttle
And it's a hard place to escape from
And you're a hard case
When you're on your way down

See the blue boy
Under the silver moon
He can't see her
Though she's right there in the room

So he strolls downtown
To the drowning places
Get the whiskey down ya boy
Paint a smile upon the faces
But he's not free tonight
Chorus To look at the love upon that face
To look at the light she throws upon a darkened place
To look at the world that bore her
To look at the hands before her
To look at the love upon that face

So he sings his song
With soul on the strings
And he's cutting his throat
With his peacocks and rings
Wild eyed and crazy
Like a raven in the night
So full of lonely and the whiskey bite
I found these words today
Among my masterpieces
Something I scrawled out
For my Masters thesis
As for this hopeless liquid philosophy
I could justify
I just could not see

Chorus To look at the love upon that face
To look at the light she throws upon a darkened place
To look at the world that bore her
To look at the hands before her
To look at the love upon that face

Education

'Education is the most powerful weapon which you
can use to change the world.'

Nelson Mandela

According to Kofi Annan: 'Knowledge is power. Information is liberating. Education is the premise of progress, in every society, in every family.'

When it comes to life in general, knowledge is power. When we learn to understand ourselves and others, we tend to connect better with other human beings. We learn how to show respect and also get it for ourselves. The tools of effective interaction with the wider world become available to us.

The 'knowledge is power' quote is one that applies to overcoming addiction, whether it is for the individual or the family. To learn and apply knowledge is not easy but it can be life-changing. The path towards recovery begins with the first step of realising and admitting that we are powerless over the substance, the behaviour or our loved one in addiction. Self-confrontation and being honest with ourselves requires much courage and strength.

When it comes to addiction, education is a powerful tool we can use to change ourselves. It is vital that we learn as much as we can about the impact of addiction on the individual and on the family. It can be all too easy to slip into denial: 'I don't drink as much as John down the road', or for the family member: 'My son/daughter will grow out of it, it's just a phase'.

When denial happens, it can stop us from moving forward. It is important to educate ourselves so as we can understand and overcome the debilitating condition of addiction: its sources, patterns, consequences and physiological underpinnings. If you are concerned about your own relationship with alcohol, drugs, gambling, food etc., or you have someone you love that you are concerned about, check out what support services are available for your situation [see Appendix, page 259 for information].

The quest to know ourselves, the world, human nature and the universe can be a lifelong and ultimately empowering one. In order to engage in this quest, we have to open ourselves up to the changes that arise from digging beneath the surface of things, and finding the key to our true potential.

Frances

A mother writes to her son in addiction
about the process of recovery.

Dear Son

You were our first-born and you brought so much love and joy into our lives. I remember the day you were born. Your dad was so happy – he looked at me and told me how much he loved me and thanked me for giving him such a lovely baby. Those fun years seemed to slip by so quickly; I often think of how much I really do miss them. You were a wonderful child and we were so proud of you in every way. You never gave us any trouble and everyone praised you for being such a great kid.

Then, the teenage years came, and nothing could have prepared us for the changes that happened. You seemed so troubled and I worried about what was going on inside of you. You were nearly 18 before you took your first drink but you fell instantly in love with it. I guess from that day on we started to lose you more and more. You didn't want to listen to advice and all our efforts seemed to be in vain. We tried everything: talking to you; being kind and caring; being hard and tough, but nothing worked. We tried counselling and even looked at ourselves to see had we done anything to cause this. You had so much potential and you were throwing it all away.

By the time you were 19, I knew you had a drink problem and that if you didn't get help you would end up in trouble. It was a terrible time for me, the worry and fear was immense. I felt that you were falling down a cliff and I couldn't pull you back up. Night after night, waiting for you to come home . . . Hearing you vomit and seeing your health deteriorate was devastating. Two more years of struggle followed, trying everything and just ending up in the same place. You made promises that you didn't keep and played mind games with us. I thought I was going crazy at times and went from being so angry with you to the feeling of a deep grief. We were losing you and our whole family was being ripped apart.

A year ago, following the warning of being asked to leave the family home, you decided to go and talk to someone in the Rutland Centre. It was a difficult day for you, and your dad and me. I remember the counsellor saying to you that you loved drink more than your family. We all felt it, but I was given a sense of hope that you would finally do something. However, again my hopes were shattered when days later you told me you wouldn't be doing the programme.

Physically and emotionally drained, we decided to seek support for ourselves. At first, we were full of dismay, fear and guilt. But the empathy and understanding we received gave us strength. She has done so much for us over the last year that I can't thank her enough.

With the help of therapy, we have learned so much and we are now getting our lives back. Asking you to leave home was so difficult but the programme helped us to realise how important it was not to enable your addiction.

We are so proud of you today having completed the six-week Rutland programme and doing well in your recovery. We know it is your recovery and it is a great feeling that today we are able to detach from it with love.

Through The RISE and Rutland programmes, we have now met so many families who have been affected by addiction and it has been a great help being able to connect with people who understand what we are going through. Together we are all living one day at a time but we are in a much better place. I know how hard your recovery is and I do hope and pray you will continue with it and live a happy and full life. Whatever you do, I know I must stay on my own recovery, and be strong and that this will be the best help I can give you and show you how much I love you.

My love always,
Mam

Paul McGrath shares extracts from his autobiography, and writes about how he is doing today, five months sober.

Excerpt from 'Back from the Brink'

It started with Pernod and sherry. Bottles of duty-free in the room I was sharing. I was eighteen years old and on my first trip abroad. The warmth of the first swig got me interested. I needed Dutch courage. I overdid it. I had never drunk before, so this was quite a discovery. I felt something profound happen. 'Jesus, this is magnificent,' I thought. I sat there in the room experiencing this sense of calm flood through me. I began to feel invincible. I was hooked on that feeling of liberation now. I wanted more. Every night in Germany I drank. Every night, I got drunk. The drink helped me shed all feelings of self-consciousness. The voice in my head was silent.

I was lost watching the world from a mysterious perch. Every sound muffled, every picture blurred. Cast adrift in a place where I couldn't be reached. Floating. I was basically just shutting down, drifting further and further into myself. I was becoming a zombie.

Eventually, I would quite literally drink whatever I could. It started off with bottles of lager. But, later in my career I graduated to stronger stuff. Vodka, whatever. After a while, I would be conscious that I was actually drinking far too much. If I was going anywhere with

Claire, I'd have to have a few drinks before we even went outside the door. We were getting invited out a lot, going to parties all over Manchester. Claire always begged me, 'Look, please don't get drunk tonight.' I rarely listened. I'd have enough on board before we'd even arrive to be maybe just two more drinks away from drunkenness. Looking back, it was very tough for her having to put up with that.

I can still see the look of disgust on Jim's face as I launched a one-man attack on the minibar. Sitting on the edge of my bed, I went through every single drink in the fridge. Whisky, brandy, vodka, gin, wine, champagne, beer, everything. The only drinks left were the non-alcoholic stuff. And all the time I'm chatting to Jim, as if what I'm doing is the everyday act of a normal, perfectly rational human being.

Alcoholics are accomplished liars, we even lie to ourselves. Myth displaces fact. We have tales, sob stories and excuses almost on tap. Deep down, of course, I know I've fucked up again. I've let people down. And letting people down is like pulling a trigger. As of now, I'm running away. That night I slip into whatever company I can find. I drink everything, smoke everything, take everything that's offered. My head is all over the place. There's too much going on in my life. Too much secrecy and lies. Drink is the gaffer now. I had been drinking non-stop for a week, yet all I wanted now was another one. Something to blur things. To numb the sense of shame.

I could always press the abort button and just pour away this dangerous, clear liquid that now has my rapt attention. But I won't. I have a desire to be numbed, a need to feel safe in the warm glow. Four large vodkas. The key to being normal. I swallow them down, giddy and guilty and definitely scared. As of now, the night ahead is a great, black mystery. Where will it take me? Who will pick up the pieces? Will I come through alive?

The room was pitching and rolling. I felt hopelessly tired. Lying on the bed, I might as well have been on a dinghy in the ocean. Then, it seems, I got up and went missing for half an hour. Where did I go? Who knows. Probably just to a toilet somewhere to swallow a few tranquillisers. Almost certainly somewhere for a top-up. It's a horrible feeling when you know you've lost control. You're craving a heavy hit of something just to bring you back to what you perceive to be normality. And that's the weird thing. Sometimes you manage to function. Sometimes you get through it in a relatively inconspicuous way and find yourself thinking, 'that was fine today'. If you put a bottle of vodka in one hand and your kids in the other – horrible as it is to say – the alcoholic will probably go for the vodka. It's a decision you regret after the very first sip.

I felt ashamed to have let down so many people, so many children. But guilt is routine in the addict's world. It never seems powerful enough to overcome the next temptation. I mean, my own children have seen me in shocking circumstances . . . they've seen things that kids should never see. Christopher especially, he's had a front row seat for a depressing array of his dad's falls from grace. I would estimate that I've ruined at least five family holidays in my time. Holidays where I became a total mess.

When I'm sober and unmedicated, the fun we share brings me out in goosebumps. I love being able to love them. It really is that simple. To get up in the morning and think about what it is I can do as distinct from what it is I can't. The past is unchangeable. It's time to stop looking behind.

Paul McGrath writes about being sober.

Dear Reader

I am five months' sober today and I feel great. Many people mightn't think so but for me or anyone else with an alcohol addiction, this is amazing! I have come a long way from the place I was. It is hard to believe but it's true. I am happy and delighted. I feel good. Christmas was brilliant: I spent it in Crumlin with my mam. We had a really quiet, relaxing time. Christmas is supposed to be the hardest time for anyone who is not drinking, with all the parties and get-togethers, but it was fine. The snow was beautiful.

Spring is here now, and I am keeping busy and active. I make sure I fill my days and get out and about. I am developing new interests too. I realise now it is very important to fill my time well. I've been spending time in Bray with people who have suffered brain injuries – I really enjoy that. I am so grateful for all I have. I am looking after myself and things are going well.

Good things do happen. You renew and rekindle relationships, you meet new people and make new friends – I am, and it's a very good feeling.

I am very open about my troubles with addiction, having written about the ups and downs of my life in my autobiography – I think this has been good for me, and besides, I prefer my children to hear the correct version as opposed to how the press put things!

And this book you are reading now is another opportunity to be open, to reach out, to help anyone with addiction issues, and there are lots and lots of us out there. When I was playing football, a lot of the other players thought I was being a prima donna when I was drinking and playing – they didn't understand that I just couldn't stop myself and I wasn't 'just acting up'. Very few around me (including myself) understood the nature of alcohol addiction, and things were different back then too. Management were okay with what I was doing as long as I 'sort of' kept it all on an even keel (there isn't really such a thing). I was still playing well so I got away with a lot. Developing greater awareness and providing proper support services to those suffering from addiction and people living with addiction is so important because addiction is impacting so many lives in such a severe way, particularly in Ireland.

But for me today – it's good, the sun is shining and I am happy and optimistic, thank God! I'll just keep going the way I am going and it will be okay.

Paul

Words from Paul's mother and eldest son, excerpted from 'Back from the Brink'.

Betty McGrath: I am an elderly woman now, praying every day for my son's health and happiness. Sometimes, when he is missing, I wish for selfish things. I wish he was sitting before me in the front room, drinking even. Better he'd drink in the security of home than find himself cut adrift among strangers who probably only care for his celebrity value. I suppose I live a lot on my nerves now. I worry endlessly about Paul. I worry about someone taking advantage. I worry about him being hurt physically. When he doesn't ring me, I always fear the worst. But I believe Okune (Paul's sister who died in 1994) is on his shoulder . . . she is his guardian angel.

Christopher McGrath: I know he feels guilty about us. He thinks that he's put us through hell and back. But we're fine. We deal with it in our own sort of way. He's got the love from all of us. He knows that. We just want him to have a happy life, to be obviously teetotal. Above anything to be well because when he's well, we're all well.

A mother writes to her daughter in rehab.

Dear Daughter

You are in rehab as I write. I'm looking about our living room. There are three photographs of you on display.

In the first, you are about three. You are in my arms, our faces almost touching. We are not looking at the camera. We are discussing something out of the camera's view. I don't remember what now. The picture captures a loving mother-and-child moment.

The second is a full family photo, taken on the day of me and your dad's fortieth wedding anniversary. I look so happy and proud of my children, including you, the young woman in the Kate Moss dress. I have studied your face closely, but can see no sign that, two years on, you would be frail and unkempt. Worse than that, that you would be addicted, self-centred, deceitful – someone I didn't know, didn't want to be with.

The last picture you gave me about six months ago, saying it was one of the few happy days you had in a long time. It was taken the last time you were in rehab.

I went recently to Rathlin Island. It was there I came to understand that I can look at that family photo and know that I did the best I could for you. I did not cause your addiction. I cannot cure it either. You are an adult and have to make your own choices.

I am your mother. I love you. Now go and live your life and let me live mine.

Your Mum

A woman recounts her experience of her ex-husband's addiction throughout their relationship.

Dear Husband

We were still teenagers when we met first met. Ten years later we married, making a vow to love and honour, for richer, for poorer, in sickness and health all the days of our lives. I fulfilled all of that, except the last part! When we first met, you were full of confidence, with a certain swagger and plenty of money in your pocket. You were fond of a drink, almost your entire social life centred on the pub. To go in at lunchtime on a Saturday, and stay until closing was not unusual, except to go home to your mother for dinner just across the road. On Sundays the pub opened its doors at 12.30 – you would head home for the 'Holy Hour', then back until closing. Any other interests usually incorporated a drink. When you were in your twenties, you were well able to hold your alcohol. You never appeared drunk; you were invariably amiable and well-mannered, and could be relied upon to keep a cool head in a fraught situation.

Moving on ten years. You were a good husband and a good father to our small children. I became increasingly unwell, anxious and very unhappy. I had suffered depression as a teenager. I went back to my psychiatrist to seek help. Soon after, I began to have an inkling of your addiction problem, but thought I was making too big a thing of it. Perhaps I didn't want to see it for what it was . . .

For the past ten years, my life has been varying degrees of a nightmare, sheer unadulterated hell. A web you drew me into without me even realising. Your addiction really took hold. The alcohol brought out a very, very nasty side of you. While never violent, your verbal abuse was absolutely appalling! The effect on my self-esteem, self-confidence and security was immeasurable. Words could never express my pain and despair. You very nearly crushed me.

I can remember that awful sense of shame, and I couldn't tell anyone what was happening. I felt so hopeless, helpless, terrified. What would happen to me and my children? I was a stay-at-home mother. Money was tight but, after 13 years out of the workforce, I got a job. It was like starting again. It was only part-time, but it gave me some independence and also self-confidence.

My psychiatrist helped me to see and acknowledge to myself what was happening. Helped me to see your addiction and the very serious detrimental effects both on me and our children. As the addiction took hold, it was impossible not to have confrontations with you. No matter what I did or said (or didn't do or didn't say), there was a row. I was always in the wrong, you believed.

Finally, I decided I'd had enough. I went about getting a separation. I had gone to solicitors four times previous to this. Each time I was told it would cost too much, that there was not enough to split financially, that the emotional costs would be too high. This time though I had to do it. For my own and the children's sake I had to carry it through. You had also had to hit rock bottom.

During this time, it was suggested to me that I attend a course at The RISE Foundation. There I joined a group of all ages, whose friends and relatives all had various addictions. To listen to their stories was a revelation! I discovered I was not the only one to feel the many emotions that I had gone through. To talk to people who had had similar experiences brought peace and understanding. I was helped to understand the many co-dependencies of addiction.

Eventually, our separation. The pain of that day will never leave me, the utter desolation. Where had all those dreams of going through life together gone? They have been so cruelly shattered. The scars on me and our children will last a lifetime.

Dear Husband, I am still concerned about you. You are the father of our children. I hope you find your own path and can live your life without alcohol, in the real world.

Always remember

Y*ou will survive. Be stronger.*

Good luck
Your Ex-Wife

*A woman describes her own journey
to recovery as a family member.*

My father was a very big drinker. We lived in a town near many public houses and he would spend every evening after work and weekends in one of them. When he was drunk he was very aggressive; he often got into fights and would arrive home with cuts and grazes on his face, and he would still be fighting! Although my mother would try to get us to bed early so that we wouldn't hear him shouting, it was just a small little flat – sure, everyone on the road could hear him coming up the stairs.

From as far back as I can remember, I've always felt a huge responsibility for my family. I would try my absolute best to resolve any problems. Five of us shared a little bedroom and if there was a lot of shouting and violent behaviour in the house, I would try and reassure my younger brothers and sisters that everything was ok. I would make up imaginary games, like getting them to close their eyes and pretend that we were watching TV. 'What station are you watching?' I'd shout to my little brother. 'Great cartoon on RTÉ!' 'Right, lets change over the channels now.' Silly little games that made no sense at all, but it was just something to take their minds off the problems outside, until they fell asleep.

If I had a problem at school or out on the street with other kids, I'd never tell. I just didn't want to add to my mother's problems. I tried so hard to be a really good kid. I got on well in school and was exceptionally good at sports and art, winning many medals and certificates – I really loved making my mother proud.

As I got older, my feelings of being responsible for the welfare of my family grew more and more. I got part-time jobs and used every penny I earned on my brothers and sisters, buying them goodies and bringing them out to the local cinema or the zoo. I could never understand why my friends didn't do this – instead they would buy the latest fashions or use their money to get drink at the weekends and hang around the park. But I was quite happy just to head home with a bag full of little surprises.

I'd help Mam paint and wallpaper, and did a lot of jobs that our neighbours' husbands did, like fixing punctures on bikes or fixing things around the house – it was all just part of my normal routine.

At 20, I met my now-husband and I was shocked at his reaction to how much I did for my family. He had travelled a lot and wasn't as attached to his family at all. They met up often and got on very well but they were all very independent and were all just getting on with their own lives. I thought that was very strange and I couldn't stop feeling the way I did. I just thought that my mother and my brothers and sisters were very close, much closer than his family were. I was always defending the relationship we had and the amount of time I spent with them. If my family needed money I felt obliged to lend it to them. By this stage I was earning a good wage so it wasn't a problem. If any of my siblings found themselves in any trouble I'd be the one to sort if out.

Eventually they all grew up but I still insisted on being

a huge provider of support to them. I was always trying to please them and make their lives easier. I was their first point of contact if my father was behaving badly – I would go around and fight with him, sometimes physically, which I now regret.

So when the problems with my sister arose I immediately took over trying to 'fix her'. She had been doing really well in her job but, when her friend confided in me that she was really worried about her drinking. I was there immediately to solve it all.

I sat talking to her for hours, trying to figure out what we were going to do – I felt so sad and hurt for her. I took her into my house, trying to mother her, much to the disapproval of my husband, but I convinced him that this was just a temporary arrangement.

Things got slightly better for a while but it wasn't long before she was out of control again. This time I found that she was taking prescription tablets and drink together – a disastrous combination.

I spent hours researching rehabilitation places, driving her to different centres for counselling, all the time failing to notice that my own family were suffering. My husband was at his wit's end; when he tried to talk to me I would become defensive and angry – what was I supposed to do, just leave her in her flat to die on her own?!

I neglected not only my husband, but my own children and my friends – I'd make excuses for why I couldn't go out to meet them. I slowly drifted away into my own world.

Treatment centre after treatment centre . . . the years passed and every relapse just got worse and worse. I was a failure. How could I not sort my baby sister out? I now had lots of other problems on my plate too!

I found my job harder; my boss was very unhappy with my absenteeism and my productivity. My husband was distant and seemed to be busier than ever, going out all the time and getting on with his own life. My kids were much the same.

I started to resent my sister, especially when the suicide threats came. When I'd pull back from her, there'd be calls at all hours of the day and night. At this stage she knew the inside of every treatment centre, general and mental hospital on this island.

Terrible thoughts went through my head – I often wished she was dead and then I would be filled with such remorse for thinking like that. I began to hate myself.

Why did I feel so responsible for her? On the few occasions that I did try and speak to friends about the situation, they'd empathise with me and tell me about their 'Uncle Joe' or 'mad Auntie Jane'. But that still didn't solve my problem! They just couldn't understand why I felt I had to take on so much responsibility. 'What about your brother? What about your mother? She's not your responsibility, she's a grown woman.'

I couldn't sleep, I just couldn't relax. I had this huge weight on my shoulders and a pain that wouldn't go away.

The change came when I saw an ad for The RISE Foundation and reluctantly decided to go. Even walking through those doors that night, my main thought was that maybe someone here would have the answer to solving my sister's problems.

But as soon as the lessons were presented to me on co-dependency and the 'roles' children take on in families with addiction problems, I just could not believe my ears. All at once everything fell into place, it all began to make perfect sense. How could this person presenting know so much about *me*?! How had I not heard about this stuff before?! I cried, I felt as if I was going to faint at times. I was just so overcome with all this *new* information.

I had never wanted to do group therapy or peer support. I just didn't like the idea. Sorry, I forgot to mention earlier that I'm very stubborn. Also, I absolutely didn't like the idea of telling anyone the truth about my family. That was family business and I should not 'wash my dirty linen in public'! Sure, how could I trust these strangers anyway?

But I was so overcome by the lessons at the beginning of each session in the programme that I found it easy to stay for the group therapy session. We weren't sitting there moaning, all we were doing was discussing the lesson and how we identified with it, and from that came the rest – The Healing. It was powerful: we cried, we laughed, we cursed at times and slowly but surely the guilt, the pain began to lift from my chest.

I was sitting in a room with the loveliest people I'd ever met, all who felt the exact feelings that I had felt. Through the lessons and the group therapy I began to let go.

I know it's hard to believe but my life has changed. I no longer feel the same need to fix people; I don't feel the same responsibility for my sister; I look at things completely differently now. I am lucky that this was also a very good experience for my husband and that he is still around!! He actually admitted to me later that he had contemplated leaving. But he's happy with the changes he can see in me. I can book a holiday or little break away now without the worry, stress and guilt that I used to feel.

My only regret is that I didn't get to do this years ago. I've lost a lot of time that I can't get back but I am certainly going to try and make up for it with my family.

I keep in touch with my sister but I have boundaries now – she has had to learn to fend for herself a bit better and she's coping. I've learned to verbalise: to put my thoughts into words, to speak to her about my worries for her. I'm able to tell her I love her, and I'm able to get on with my life and not feel guilty.

Boundaries

'The purpose of having boundaries is to protect and take care of ourselves. We need to be able to tell other people when they are acting in ways that are not acceptable to us.'

From Co-dependence: The Dance of Wounded Souls
by Peter Jordan

Why do we need to set boundaries? When it comes to the issue of addiction it is vital to put them in place. Boundaries help us to decide who we are in relation to other people. They are a major component to ensuring healthy relationships and personal growth. When we have a loved one in addiction, establishing healthy boundaries can be challenging.

We set these boundaries so we can stop enabling our loved one and help them move closer to change. If we don't set boundaries then they may take advantage of the situation. If we do not set positive limits on what they can and cannot do, then they will not get any closer to change in their life.

Setting appropriate boundaries will not only help the family members but may also help the person in addiction. Boundaries bring order to our lives, strengthen our relationships with others and ourselves, and are essential to our mental and physical health. The purpose of having boundaries is to protect and take care of ourselves. We need to be able to tell other people when they are acting in ways that are not acceptable to us. Setting boundaries can be difficult for the family member as they may have adapted to the behaviour of the person in addiction, so it takes practice. That is why it is important to seek support and guidance when dealing with this sort of situation. The family member may find that the best place to get that advice is from other people who have gone through the same thing, as their experience can benefit them directly.

The person in addiction may not stop acting in addiction unless they are facing a major negative consequence.

The point of setting boundaries is to nudge our loved one in addiction to the moment of surrender. It is only through pain that they will arrive there. They cannot start to feel good until they decide to make the intense, life-altering changes that are needed in order to live sober. This is a really big deal and a huge commitment. They may not do this unless they have no other choices and they are completely miserable because of their addiction. That is the only path out of addiction and by setting boundaries it encourages the person in the cycle of addiction to begin to walk that path.

Appropriate boundaries create integrity, and open up the possibility of breaking the cycle of addiction and co-dependency.

Frances

A woman writes to her younger self, and tells her story

Dear 16-Year-Old Self

Hi there

Just wondering where and how you are? I haven't seen you for a while. The last time I saw you, you had just left Belfast, with help from your brother, and you were starting a new life in Newry. You were working two jobs, had new friends and were living life for you.

Before you arrived in Newry, you had been going through a difficult time. When you were 12, your mother and father split up and your mother's drinking got much worse. You had been looking after your younger brother and sisters for a few years, keeping the house together, making sure nobody knew how bad things had really become with your mother's drinking. Before, it would only happen a few times a year; now it was nearly every fortnight, for three or five days at a time. This woman who was so kind and honest got lost. She couldn't cope with her life. She would make sure dinner was ready, uniforms washed, plenty of food in the house, so she could escape into her world of drink. While she was in her world, your world fell apart. You had to be Mammy and Daddy to your siblings. Because she had so much hate in her, it would be taken out on you. If people asked about your home life, you would always lie – social services, family, teachers, anybody who asked questions.

Do you remember the day you had had enough? Your brother, who was two years younger but always stronger, said matter-of-factly, 'That's it!' You both left and walked the miles to a friend's house, along back roads so you wouldn't be spotted. When you arrived it was late, you were hungry and she tried to help us. She called your father and you asked him to come and get you because you couldn't stay with Mammy any longer. He came and took you to Newry. A few days later, the phone rang. It was Mammy. She was very sorry, upset, guilty and asking, begging for you to go back to her. You gave in. Nothing lasts forever. Again and again she would slip. Eventually, you got strong and you stayed, got a job, made friends and had your own life.

Your father was always taking you camping to a beautiful place in Donegal with your brother and sometimes your sisters. This was handy for him as he could relax and know you were all ok and safe. He had no bother with you all.

So, 16-year-old girl, finally free, no worries, no hassles, how could you have known that chapter two in your difficult journey was just about to unfold?

I met Johnny when I was 17, at a concert. He came up to me. 'Hello Maire,' he said. I recognised him from that beautiful place in Donegal, even though I had never spoken to him before. Here was a man who was good to me. After a year, I fell pregnant. Despite pressure from my mother to get married before the child was born, we decided to wait. I must have had some inkling then that Johnny had a drink problem because I asked him to promise that our child would not be brought into an alcoholic family. He promised.

Within six months I turned 19, had our son and moved to Donegal where I didn't really know anybody. I'd be left at home with the baby while he headed out. I was very lonely. When we did go out together, I would get so excited. He would drink loads and leave me, but luckily in time I did make my own friends.

As the years went by, I learned to go out on my own. Johnny wouldn't talk in the house and I needed company. I would suggest turning off the TV or going away for a while together, and though he'd agree, this would never happen. Then I was told by the doctor that I had a problem and couldn't have any more children. But I didn't give up and was overjoyed when I discovered I was pregnant. But I miscarried and, while I was in the hospital, I knew that things were getting out of control with Johnny's drinking. Soon after, I started to control things so he couldn't drink.

Happily I got pregnant again and gave birth to our baby daughter, followed two years later by another son. But Johnny was drinking so much more now, and rows had become more and more frequent. Then, one night, I started a row and he stormed out. I knew he had drink with him. Six hours later and no sign of him. I knew there was something wrong and decided to call the police. Luckily, he was found after he had fallen into a ditch at the side of the road. He was lucky. It was a freezing cold night.

From then we would both row, and sometimes I would

leave and Johnny would stop drinking, but never for long. Finally a friend came and said enough was enough and gave him the number of a treatment centre. He attended and it helped him stay off the drink, for a few years. But it was nearly worse. There was no communication, not until he started drinking again. This time, he was way out of control, even going to work drunk. He finally agreed to a six-week recovery programme.

After he'd been sober for a while, I agreed he could take the kids on holiday to Spain. The final straw was a call from one of my children asking me to come over and get her. 'Daddy is drinking again.' It hit me then that it was nearly the same call I had made all those years ago to your own daddy. The pattern had come full circle.

Sixteen-year-old self, can you find me, so we can be there again?

*A sister tells of how, in just a single year,
her brother's drug addictions took hold and sent the
lives of her family members spiralling into chaos.*

Somehow it wasn't registering with my brother in quite the same way as it was with the rest of us. It was like it was all new to him. He was shocked at these events taking place around him: 'She wants me out?', 'Everybody is ganging up on me', 'That friend of hers never liked me.' Everyone else was to blame and it went on and on, the explanations becoming more elaborate and creative. At times, he was totally convincing, but if one audience copped on and began to question and confront him, he would back off and find someone new to try and convince, after all he had convinced *himself*!

Once upon a time, he had held it all together. He worked hard during the week, well able to multi-task and impress the boss. The younger siblings really enjoyed his company and looked up to him. He did always like to party – sometimes he would fall asleep sitting up, or he might need a link on the way home, but it wasn't a problem. But then he discovered coke – he could 'keep it together' and drink more. The hangovers lasted longer, but nothing a sleeping tablet or a Valium couldn't sort out. He could get these as easily as cocaine. He became secretive about what he was taking. Eventually, it was no longer about the drink. It was all coke – it was getting out of control.

He started getting sloppy in work, and soon he couldn't

hold down a job. Then, he was living off sick benefit, and getting prescriptions from a number of unsuspecting doctors in the area. His family life suffered, and his paranoid episodes became so bad that, on one occasion, worried he was a danger to himself, we were forced to call an ambulance. But when the ambulance came, he wouldn't go. What do you do then? Call a doctor? How do you call a psychiatrist? The fear, frustration, anger and upset is just so difficult to put into words. Never mind the embarrassment with all the neighbours watching like it was some horrible scene from a soap opera.

Nothing seemed to slow him down. We all had our opinions, or approaches to what we should do, and this led to tension in the family. His wife was at her wit's end. We were spending hours and hours on the phone; this problem was not going away. My siblings and I had suffered as children through my father's alcohol addiction – he was very violent at times – and some of the frustrations we were now feeling had been suppressed from years earlier. We thought we had left this behind a long time ago. We hated my brother for making my mother cry again, like she had when we were children.

We would get calls at all hours of the day and night, you'd never know what was coming next. No matter how much you try to not let it affect your own family, it does!

Eventually, it did come to a head. With a bit of pressure, he did leave his family home. We brought him to my mother's home, and, over two weeks, tried to detox him. It wasn't easy, especially for my mother, but eventually he did come round and we could talk to him – he was listening. We were very lucky that we had help from counsellors in our area and the local priest called in frequently and spoke to him on the phone.

Slowly he began to realise that the only way forward was to get help. He could see what he had lost, and was still losing. But 'getting help' wasn't easy. The priest in our area was always saying that there should be a treatment bed available for every person who admits that they want help immediately – because if the bed is not available at that moment, we lose them again and then it's too late. I know exactly what he means now.

Eventually my brother did get help, and he did manage to stay sober. For a while. When he relapsed, all hell broke loose. I was exhausted by now, mentally and physically.

I eventually made the decision to walk away. It was not an easy decision, especially when my mother remained co-dependent. We are a very close family and his behaviour was tearing us apart. Eventually I found support: I discovered The RISE Foundation. I signed myself and my mother up. The Family Programme was powerful: it was extremely helpful to hear professionals talking about addiction, detachment, co-dependency, the effects on families and relationships, the shame, the stigma. And *recovery* – not only for the addict, but for *me*! It was a relief to hear that I was not mad or a bad person for having the feelings I had. I was carrying huge guilt. There were times during the programme that were not easy. I had to look at myself, my past, my behaviour, but it is all part of recovery and it does work. I have taken the first step on a new journey and I plan to continue.

Looking back, it was the best thing I could do, and my brother is in recovery again – which is great.

A wife writes to her husband in addiction about her decision to seek help.

When I met you that first time, I knew you were the one. When you looked into my eyes, the chemistry was so strong that I actually felt my knees go weak. I didn't know what was happening to me – I had never felt this way before. I couldn't believe that, of all the beautiful girls that were there, you chose to dance with me. I thought I was floating as we moved around the dance floor. I was 17 and you were 19. We were both from a small town but I had never seen you before. You had been away at boarding school and then college, and were now home for the summer to work with your dad at his very successful business. I knew of your family, as they were the wealthiest family in the town.

When the dance ended, you looked into my eyes and said, so quietly and politely, that you would like to walk me home. This time, I held your gaze for a moment, and when I looked into your blue eyes, I saw they were tinged with sadness. I felt a feeling that I had never felt before: I was going to help you. I was going to do everything in my power to make you happy. I was going to fix everything for you.

We started going out and I thought I had died and gone to heaven. Again, I couldn't believe you had chosen me as there were so many other beautiful girls in our town, and here I was, with my dark-red, curly hair, green eyes and freckles, with you. You were tall with dark, soft, curly hair and the most amazing bright-blue eyes.

You always liked your few pints and a little flutter on the horses, but then who didn't? At the time I was so blinded by my feelings for you that I never really noticed that there was always a smell of drink on your breath. I kind of got used to it.

I got pregnant quite soon after we met. I had just turned 18. When I told you I was pregnant, you just said that we had better get married. You were very matter-of-fact about it all, and didn't seem to care either way. As for me, this was it; all my dreams were coming true. I was going to have my baby with the man of my dreams. I was on cloud nine and I didn't care what anyone thought of us. It was all organised, we would get married quickly with no fuss and we would move into the little cottage that was on your dad's land.

On the day of the wedding, you arrived at the small church outside our town very drunk. I couldn't believe it when I walked up the aisle and I could smell the alcohol. Immediately, my heart sank, but I pretended to myself that you hadn't been drinking. I put on a brave face as you got worse throughout the day. I just kept smiling at people as they would look at me with sympathetic eyes. By eight o'clock that night, you had to be put to bed with a basin by your side. This wasn't a good ending to the fairytale wedding that I had dreamed of all my life.

So that was the beginning of my journey as your wife.

Life went on and somehow I got myself into a routine around your drinking and gambling. The only time I felt ok was when you were at work because I knew you were safe there. You never missed a day at the family business, but when work finished, that is when my anxiety and my obsessive thinking would start. You would go to the pub and get drunk. I would spend my evening calling you on your phone; when you wouldn't answer, I would call all the pubs to see where you were. Sometimes you would drive to other pubs in other towns so I couldn't contact you. Then, I would call my sister, mother, any of my family members to come and babysit for me so I could go looking for you. When I found you drunk in a pub somewhere, I would take you home. You never argued with me. You would just keep saying you were sorry as I screamed and shouted at you.

By the time I was in my mid-twenties we had a family of four beautiful children: two boys and two beautiful girls. When I look back now, I realise that those wonderful children lost not only their dad to addiction, they lost me too. My obsession with where you were and what you were doing drove me insane, and there is no way I could have been present to them. You were all I could think of. Constantly wondering if you would go off with some other woman in the town. Would you lose all our money at the bookies? Would you crash the car and kill yourself? The worst thought of all was: would you kill someone else?

I now believe that I was actually sicker than you at that time. The anger that I felt towards you and your drinking was toxic for me, and I feel this anger impacted our children more than your drinking did. Somehow, they seemed to accept your behaviour but were more upset and worried about the way I was. I was constantly angry and constantly trying to control you and your behaviour, but to no avail. You just couldn't hear me because you were in oblivion and you didn't want to hear me.

I stopped eating because I had a constant knot in my stomach from the anger and anxiety. I stopped sleeping. Eventually this took its toll on me: I collapsed and was taken to hospital. They kept me in for a few days, put me on a drip for dehydration and got me physically strong enough to go home. When I got home, I realised that I had to make some changes in my life. Looking at our children's frightened faces, as they thought I was going to die, had churned something up inside me. The one thing I knew was that I didn't want us to split up. I still loved you with all my heart. I still felt the same way about you as I did the night we met, but I knew something needed to change for me.

I got on the internet and looked up what families can do when living with someone who has a problem with alcohol. I found it difficult to accept that you were an alcoholic as my idea of an alcoholic was somebody living on the streets, with no job and no family. The funny thing was that you kept working through your extreme drinking. I now know that sometimes for an alcoholic the last thing to go for them is their job. They may lose their partner, their children, their home but they will hold on to their job until the end.

I decided that I would travel to Dublin for one night a week to learn how to deal with what was going on in my home. Dare I say it, to learn how to deal with your addiction. It was a family programme that was held for ten weeks. It was life-changing for me. I learned that I was powerless over your drinking and gambling behaviour. I learned that I was enabling you to stay in your addiction because I was always picking up the pieces for you. I learned I had to detach from your addictive behaviour; I learned I had to set boundaries. This was difficult but I was determined and I felt great support from the group to do this.

I really took on board what I learned. I became more present to my children. I worked hard at not obsessing about you. I worked hard at letting go of my anger towards you.

Now, a year down the line of my recovery, you came to me yesterday and said you wanted to stop drinking and gambling. You asked me if I would help you, and, of course, I said yes. We have an appointment next week for an assessment at a treatment centre in Dublin. I am happy for you that you have made this decision, and I feel hopeful that we may have the life together that I always dreamed of. I am not so naive to believe that it is going to be easy, but I believe that if I stay on my journey of recovery, everything will be ok, no matter what.

Businessman Ben Dunne writes on his own experiences with addiction, and the power of openness.

Words to anyone out there looking to help themselves

As I write these few words, I am acutely aware that there are so many people out there, suffering. They may have an addiction or a close association with addiction, or they may simply be stressed and anxious about things and it's making life really difficult for them.

Here I am now, nigh on 20 years on after my own troubles became very public and my own recovery began. I feel very lucky. I am still happily married and I have wonderful relationships with my wife and my four children, whom I adore. While I respect the privacy of my family and my children, my openness about my own past, my addiction problems, my recovery and, well, just dealing with the things I had to address both mentally and physically, has been a big part of it for me. You see, secrecy is such a big part of addiction, it's a bad formula – and openness, well, it's just the opposite. Though the bigger reason I like to be so open and speak so frankly, even to this day, is because in some way, however small, I know I am helping somebody going through similar stuff. People who live with addiction need hope, a glimmer of light. I hope I offer a little bit of that. I'm a people person at heart. I like people.

There is such stigma attached to addiction and even more so to mental health issues in Ireland. It seems to be the modern-day leprosy! For the life of me I don't know why. Mental illness is so prevalent. When we develop a health issue (however it manifests itself), we need help to find out what the problem is and to fix it. If you have a sore leg, you go to a doctor; if you have a weak heart, you visit a cardiologist; if you have toothache, you visit a dentist – and so if you have troubles on your mind, you go to – yes – a psychiatrist or a counsellor.

It's ok to be anxious every now and again, but if you are waking up and going to sleep with the same anxieties (whether they are addiction-related or not), you need to seek help and do something about it – and there's not a thing wrong with that.

Nobody sets out to become an addict; it creeps up on you. And it can happen to anybody. It's a dreadful place to be, a most unhappy life to be living – it's rock bottom! And rock bottom is very different from one person to the next. Counselling and mental therapy help you uncover what's caused you to end up where you are and deal with the source of the problem. For me, I was sent into rehab in the US by a court order, and it was the best thing that happened to me. For others, they must choose to seek help voluntarily. That's hard. And families living with addiction need help to get better too, to learn about the nature of addiction – because living with it causes massive stresses and anxieties.

When I went into counselling, in my group, we were told to look around. The facts were that two out of three of us would not be here in five years time if we didn't smell the coffee and realise we each had to change. That really struck a chord with me. Through my counselling, I realised my own stresses were related to working in the family business. Everyone is different, but for me that was the thing that caused me so much stress, and that stress led me down the road to addiction. If I wanted to kick cocaine, I had to change my work situation. And I did change it, and the lovely thing about it is that I have now developed normal sibling relationships with my brothers and sisters. It is better for me.

During my recovery, it took some time for certain friends and family to trust in me again – or believe in me, if you will. I remember when I was going off on a business trip, someone I love asked me to promise to never take cocaine again – and I didn't know how to answer that. But through my counselling, I learned it was ok not to make that promise because I actually couldn't. I guess that's where family counselling comes in useful – loved ones of addicts learn that you can't ask that question and expect to get the answer you want. My answer, which I became ok with (and so did they), was: 'Listen, I can't even promise you I'll be here in a year. I could get run over by a bus tomorrow!'

As the years have gone by, I am no longer over-sensitive anymore. Of course, I am respectful to those I love but I am less concerned about what people think and, in a way, that in itself instils confidence in others. All I know is that when I look after myself, everything around me is and will be ok. If someone asks me now, 'How are you keeping, Ben?', I just think it's a nice thing to ask and I tell them I'm great with the same warmth with which it was intended. I never wonder anymore are they asking about you know what . . . For me, this is a sign of how far I have come.

But I still look after myself, just as everyone should do (and so many people just don't). I am happy out but I know my needs, so every so often I take off. I go away by myself to a place of quietness and beauty. In nature, I get away from the business and the busyness that is my life. It's fantastic. I love the stars there. I am miles away from everything but I'm not totally tuned out. I can still log on and take some phone calls but I'm so far away and it's so different. That's my meditation, my soul food. I come back renewed and refreshed. I come back to myself.

All the best,
Ben

On an important day, a young woman remembers how, as a child, she tried to protect her brothers from finding out about their mother's drinking.

Today is a very special day for me, and it's a day I want to remember for the rest of my life.

I come from a relatively middle-class area in the suburbs of Dublin. I was the only girl with an older and a younger brother. My father worked hard to send us to good schools and colleges. My relationship with my mother was always strained. I was the one that was most aware of her secret drinking. I tried to protect my brothers from finding out, but I believe they knew all along and played along with the secrecy. When I was eleven, I would run home from school as quick as I could, so I could tidy up the empty bottles of wine that were in the sitting room. I would try to get Mam up to bed and get some dinner on before the boys got home, and just pretend we were a normal family. It would never work out like that though because sometimes Mam would start fighting and say that I was ashamed of her. She would slur her words and stagger around the kitchen, shouting that she had nothing to hide. The boys would come home and when they walked in the door, I could see the disappointment and sadness in their faces.

We did our best as children to try and pretend everything was normal. We all believed that if we could be really good children then maybe Mam would love us enough to stop drinking, but it never worked out that way. When I would hear Dad turning the key in the front door, I'd run to greet him and he knew by my face if Mam had been drinking or not. She wouldn't drink every day – sometimes when we came home from school, we would know when she wasn't drinking because the radio was on and we could smell the aroma of our dinner cooking. They were great days: when the boys came home we'd all hug each other with joy, but those days got less and less as we got older.

My mam was a lovely woman really. She was never violent towards us; she was just sad and always crying. I felt she needed to be taken care of, and that was my role. I did my best to mind her. I think the saddest part of it all for me was watching my dad go through the loneliness and heartache. He was constantly thinking of her. He would ring me at home every half hour asking 'How is she now?' and I would say 'She's the same, Dad'. Sometimes I wished he would ask how I was.

Mam's drinking got worse, and when I was 17 (I was in the middle of doing my Leaving Cert) I came home to find she had fallen down the stairs. When I saw her lying in the hallway at the bottom of the stairs, with blood coming from her head, I thought she was dead. I rang the ambulance and then my dad. They both got to the house at the same time. Still thinking she was dead, I was hysterical. They checked her heartbeat and thankfully she was still alive. Dad went to the hospital with her. I wanted to go too but I was told to stay home to tell the boys what happened. It was the longest wait ever. Not knowing if she was going to survive, if she would be brain-damaged or in a wheelchair.

Hours later, Dad called and said she was going to be ok. There was no lasting damage. My brothers and I just looked at each other, and none of us spoke but we all knew what the other was thinking, 'When will it happen again?'

That night, my dad came home and said that Mam would be going into a treatment centre for six weeks when she got out of hospital. They would help her stop drinking. We all got so excited; I cried and so did my younger brother.

Mam went in two weeks later and we were asked to go in as her concerned persons. We would sit in a group scenario with two therapists and talk as honestly as we could about how Mam's drinking affected us as children. It was really hard to think about doing this to Mam, but we were told that Mam wasn't aware of how her drinking impacted us, and if she could hear it from us now it would help her with her recovery.

I was prepared to do anything to help her, so I went to the group and, for the first time in my life, I spoke out about what it was like for me and my brothers watching my mam drinking herself into oblivion. The therapists were lovely and very gentle with me. My mam cried a lot. The therapist asked Mam why she was crying and she just said that she wasn't aware of the devastation her drinking had caused us. She said she was really sorry. The therapist then said to Mam: 'Would you like to give your daughter a hug?' We both stood up and walked to the middle of the floor, and she put her arms around me and gave me a huge hug. We both cried and at last I felt I had got my mam back.

Mam is now eight years sober. When she came out of that treatment centre she threw herself into recovery. Myself and my brothers were advised to go to ACOA meetings – this stands for Adult Children of Alcoholics. I found these meetings really beneficial. I learned that I didn't have to be my mam's caretaker anymore. At the beginning of her recovery I found I was becoming controlling: making sure she was going to meetings and checking up on her a lot. This was very unhealthy for both me and Mam. I learned that when addiction comes into the family, there is a lot of unhealthy enmeshment and it is important to detach from old behaviours.

So, today I am getting married. I feel like the luckiest woman in the world. I have a gorgeous man. My dad will be walking me up the aisle; both my brothers are groomsmen and my mam is beside me helping me get dressed. She looks beautiful, elegant and strong today, and I will be the proudest daughter in the world to have my mam sitting beside me at the top table – sober and in recovery.

A mother tells her son about her memories of his childhood and the emotional rollercoaster she and the family experienced around his addiction.

Dear Son

I was 21 years old when you were born. I couldn't believe the joy I felt when I saw you. You opened your eyes and looked straight at me and I remember thinking, 'It's just me and you now, my lovely boy'.

Your dad had left when I told him I was pregnant; we hadn't been going out that long so I wasn't heartbroken. I just knew I was going to keep you no matter what. It had been a tough pregnancy, not so much physically but emotionally. My parents were very disappointed that I had become pregnant. They felt I had let them down and were worried what would people think of their daughter being an unmarried mother with no partner. When you were born that all changed; just like me, Mam, Dad and my brother fell madly in love with you.

I managed to get a job and an apartment in the city. Mam said she would take care of you while I worked. You were a joy and so easy to mind as a baby, always smiling and laughing. I was so happy to get you in to the Gaelscoil nearby. I had put your name down and was delighted when they sent me the letter saying that you had got a place. Both you and your cousin (my brother's son) started school together. You were the same age and were both so excited to see the other children.

It was all uphill from there. I remember the first time we watched you both singing 'Away in a Manger' in the Christmas play we all cried. We were so proud. You loved school; you did so well in all your subjects. When you went into secondary school you immediately signed up to join the hurling team along with your cousin, who was now your best friend.

Life was good for us. We didn't have much money but we got by. I was delighted with your Junior Cert results; you had done so well. When you told me that everyone was going out to celebrate their results, I thought nothing of it. Looking back now, I believe that's when things started to change.

I noticed small changes, like missing hurling training sessions on Saturday mornings after being out on Friday night with friends. This was unusual as I was aware how passionate you were about hurling. You were also isolating yourself a bit more in your room. It was when you started to have problems getting up for school in the mornings that I really started to worry. You started to argue and shout when I tried to get you to go to school. I had never seen you like this; I couldn't understand what was going on.

I noticed there was money going missing from my purse. When it happened first I thought I was being forgetful and just couldn't remember where I had spent the money. But after the third and fourth time I started to suspect you. I didn't want to believe that my lovely boy could be taking the little money that I had from me.

The mood in our home changed. I felt that you were

very hostile towards me, even though I wasn't doing anything wrong. I felt that I was walking on eggshells around you. I couldn't say anything to you without you snapping at me. It was a horrible existence and I didn't know what was happening. I thought you were depressed and asked you to go and see someone, but, again, you would snap at me and tell me to mind my own business. I felt like I was losing my beautiful boy, but I didn't know what or who I was losing you to.

I spoke with my parents who had also noticed a huge change in you, but they said it was just your hormones and you would grow out of it. Your uncle (who you adored) was also very worried; we both saw it was getting worse and you were starting to lose so much weight.

When you went out one day I went into your room to see if I could see anything that would help me understand. I knew it was wrong but I was desperate for some clue. I never went into your room as I always felt you needed your privacy, but I couldn't believe the mess I saw when I went in. I actually felt sick and was shocked that you could let it get that bad. Apart from clothes being thrown all over the floor, there was also rotten food in take-away pizza boxes, and fungus was growing in some of the cups that once had tea in them. I looked in your bedside locker and saw some empty packets. When I googled the name on the wrapper, it was clear you'd got it in a head shop. Just then I heard the door bang downstairs; I put the wrapper in my pocket and left your room. I didn't know what to do next. I knew by your behaviour, your weight loss and the mess in your room that there was something seriously wrong with you and felt that I needed to ask a professional who might know the signs of someone taking drugs.

I spent every waking moment thinking of you. I couldn't concentrate at work. I went to the doctor to get a note to take some time off. I was suffering from anxiety. When you were out, I kept thinking that I would get a phone call saying you were in hospital or dead somewhere. When you were home I was worried that you would harm yourself some way. I felt like I was living a nightmare.

I rang an organisation that deals with young people in addiction and asked them had they ever heard of this product. They told me that it contains mephedrone, and could be purchased freely in head shops. They said that it was just as dangerous to consume as cocaine or ecstasy, and it could be purchased in head shops at €17.50 for half a gram. The packet that I had seen stated that they were 'novelty bath salts only – not for human consumption'.

Here I was now with all this information and I was completely lost. What do I do? Where do I go? Should I challenge you? How much were you taking?

Where was my beautiful boy who was a wonderful student, a great hurler, and, most of all, a lovely, happy young lad? Where was my little boy who sang 'Away in a Manger' with his heart and his soul all those years ago? I really thought I was going mad, I felt so powerless. So many times I tried to talk to you and you would just lock yourself in your room.

I knew I needed help. I felt I needed some guidance, but where could I go? I rang back the centre that I had originally called and asked them where I could go to learn about living with a child who is in addiction.

They gave me a phone number. When I rang it they said they would get a counsellor to call me back. When she called me, I just blurted out the whole story to her in tears. She asked me to come in and see her.

When I went to talk to the counsellor she suggested that I do their family programme. I was prepared to do anything.

When I went along the first night I couldn't believe that there were other parents in the exact same situation as me. It was good to feel that I wasn't alone. I could identify with everything they said. They said that family members find themselves furiously searching for evidence, just like me, and that living with addiction is like being on an emotional roller coaster. The family member becomes so focused on their loved one's behaviour that they can become distracted from everything else in their lives, and that was exactly how I felt.

After I finished the family programme, I definitely felt that I had a much better understanding of addiction. I also felt so connected to the other parents that I met there. I wasn't on my own with the anxiety and fear that I was feeling. I learned that I was feeling overwhelming grief due to losing you to addiction. It was still very painful but at least I had a better understanding of it all.

One of the lectures in the programme was about intervention. I learned that intervention is the most loving, powerful and successful method yet for helping you to accept the help that you needed. I was happy to hear that family intervention could be done with love and respect in a non-confrontational, non-judgmental manner.

I learned that intervention is where the family sits down with their loved one in addiction and tries to help them to understand that they have a problem. The goal was to help you realise that you needed help. To do this, we, as a family, were to discuss possible strategies with an Interventionist who would work alongside us and guide us. So we all met with the interventionist a couple of times to do this. Your grandparents who adored you, your uncle who you looked up to all your life, and, of course, your cousin who was also one of your best friends. I felt we were doing the right thing. I just wanted to stop you from going down this horrible road of destruction.

We were all asked to write a letter to you for the intervention. It was important that the letter was concise, well-rehearsed, and from the heart.

The day arrived. I was nervous, we all were. We thought you would run out of the room. You were in the sitting room when we came in. I introduced you to the counsellor and then explained why we were all there. I could see you were restless and wanted to leave the room, but somehow you managed to stay. I knew you felt humiliated and embarrassed, and my heart went out to you, but I felt we had to continue. This was so hard but there was no other option. I read my letter first, and then the others followed. We all talked of the heartache of watching you, this beautiful young man, deteriorate in front of us.

Finally it was your cousin's turn, your best friend. We had all cried as we read out our letters but he just fell apart. He talked of how you both had played and laughed together as young lads. How he missed you being his best friend; the chats you once had about girls you fancied; the hurling matches; the laughs you had at the funny teachers you had in school. It was then that I saw something in you – you too started to cry. You said that you missed him too. You stood up and walked towards him and you both hugged each other. The counsellor than asked if you would consider getting help for your addiction and you just turned and nodded. I will never forget the words I heard when you said, 'I'm sorry I've hurt you all, I didn't know what was happening, I didn't know how to stop myself.'

You went willingly into a fantastic treatment centre for young people, and I have no doubt it was life-changing for you. I have continued on with my own family recovery. I was aware that this was important for both of us as I didn't want to smother you. I knew that it was vital that I let you go and that you take responsibility for your own recovery.

You are now one year clean and I am so proud of you.

Your Son

A mother talks about how the invasion of her family home by addiction inspired her to become 'part of the solution'.

My Journey

My journey in addiction started 14 years ago. I really can't believe it is that long ago. Time means nothing anymore. Where once my life was ruled by routines and work, I now have found myself and what I want and need to survive.

When addiction came to my family and home I was devastated. How could this happen to our family? I don't smoke or drink! We were our children's role models! How could this happen? We live in a small town; this just didn't happen outside of Dublin or London.

So, you see, I have had a long walk. At that time there were no services for families. I couldn't access help anywhere.

I have been blessed with the people I have met on my walk. I came across a family support group 40 miles from my home. I could go there and unburden myself. No one made any comment when I told them about the crazy things I was doing to try to control the chaos around me. I lived in fear. Fear that they would die, fear that I was failing them as a parent, fear that there was nothing there in the schools, doctors, HSE, clergy, gardaí, courts or addiction services to help or educate families about addiction.

As time went on, I began to see that all the services out there were as confused as I was. My family support group became my lifeline. I lived for Thursday evenings – I would have stolen a car to make sure I got to those meetings. There, I learned so much about myself! It took me to places inside myself I would never have dreamed that I could or would have dealt with. I was asked to start a support group in my area. It was great. My biggest lesson was doing a counselling course taught by William Glasser. In this discipline, I learned that everything we do, we choose for ourselves. This was a revelation to me!

For a long time, I blamed my husband for not being able to stop it, along with the community and society for allowing this to happen. Now instead of being part of the problem, I have become part of the solution. I am part of a family support network and facilitate some support groups. Even then, you can't say that you know it all and be complacent. I will be in recovery for the rest of my life and I always come across something that will keep me grateful for the blessings I have received, including the addiction. I have found the real, authentic me!

Last October, I had the great fortune to be asked to Rathlin Island with The RISE Foundation. I went but, at first, wondered what I was there for. But it turned out to be the most fantastic week. I met new people (that were walking the walk). During that time, the support, learning, food, respite and friendships were out of this world. I learned that, even though I support groups through their journeys, I need a group for me.

The foundation has everything needed to help a family to get through the devastation of addiction. It can help us to reclaim ourselves and our families, and become such a resource in our own communities. I can't thank them enough.

From a fellow traveller!

A sister's words to her sibling.

My Hero

To my darling Sister,
You were my hero,
You were everything I wanted to be
Beautiful, intelligent, slim, bubbly and confident –
Everyone wanted a piece of you
You 'had it all' – and then you had your first drink
Who were you to know, you had fallen for a vampire?

Slowly, but surely, it took away everything you ever
  had –
Your first and only real love – never to return
Your sparkling blue eyes – now blurred and reddened
Your friends – let down, time after time – just had
  enough
Your job – as your life spiralled out of control
Your self-confidence and belief – as you couldn't magic
  up the happiness you once had
Your dignity – as you drank day and night, and night
  and day
Your body – as it got sicker and sicker with every
  passing day
Thirty years and a coma later, the drink triumphantly
  took away your mind.

A simple life is left now . . . Your memory gone,
  frightened and needing full time care
But you've finally given up the demon drink –
And that is why . . .

You still have your soul
You still have your spirit
You still have your sense of humour, of belonging and
  of love
You know what happened to you and you blame no one
You are still the gorgeous, beautiful and wonderful
  woman I have always loved
We have all always loved
And you are still my hero

No longer able to remember the past, or plan for the
  future
You just live for today:
Is there any other way? – I hear you say.

With love,
Your Sis

A woman recounts her journey to recovery.

I was a child of the sixties – what an exciting time to grow up. Elvis rocked the airwaves and I was totally hooked. As Bruce Springsteen said of Elvis, 'It was like he came along and whispered a dream in everybody's ear, and then we dreamt it.' 'Free thinking' was the order of the day, and women were fighting hard for equality with men.

All was well in my life at this time and I became quite a little rebel. Behind this rebellion, however, was a shy and nervous young woman, but in my mid-twenties I found the ultimate solution for these personality discomforts: alcohol. With its help, I could rule the world.

I married at 25 and had two beautiful children before I was 30. By 42 (coincidentally the age at which Elvis died), I was a physical, emotional and spiritual wreck. My alcohol 'solution' had become an addiction that was now interfering with every aspect of my life.

I knew I was hurting my family but drowned my feelings of guilt with more alcohol. After seeing a *Late Late Show* episode which dealt with alcoholism, I decided I needed to do something about my drinking.

I went to a psychiatrist who referred me to a wonderful counsellor, who should remain nameless to save his blushes but thanks again, Rolande.

I joined a self-help group for women alcoholics which is now called ANEW. There, I found great support and a soulmate, Frances, who sadly is no longer with us. While I got so much help there, I feel there was little or no support for my family to help them through these difficult times.

During my time with ANEW, a member introduced me to the writings of Anthony DeMello and to this day I find him a constant source of enlightenment and support.

I am now 63 and have five beautiful grandchildren, the first of whom was a little girl whose constant greeting is 'I love you, Granny'. To think I might never have heard those magic words, had I continued on my downward spiral of addiction. My four other grandchildren are boys and are equally delightful.

I am content and happy now. Recovery was difficult at times but so worth all the hard work. And yes, I still sing along to Elvis and dance with my grandchildren to his intoxicating music.

A man describes how, as a child, his mother's turn on the school run filled him with anxiety.

Mum's Red Mini

The afternoon school bell would sound at 2.45 p.m. and there would always be a mad dash to put away schoolbooks, pack up bags and head for the school gates, which meant freedom for the rest of the day. Some of the older boys cycled home or took the bus, but the younger boys, like myself, were dependent on the school run i.e. a lift home from my mum or a friend's mum, depending on whose week it was.

When I knew it was my friend Stephen's mum picking us up, everything was ok and I rushed to get into the car – after all she was a 'normal mum'. When it was my mum on the school run . . . well, that was a totally different matter. From lunch-time onwards I would begin to think about it and dread the thought of her coming to pick us up. Would she be there when we got to the car park? (Always a good sign, resulting in a big sigh of relief!) Or would she be late? (Usually a bad sign that produced an ever-tightening knot in my stomach!) *Or* would she turn up at all?

Waiting for her to turn up was hell: my anxiety would grow as I wondered what kind of state would she be in? Would she embarrass me in front of my friends? What would it be like when we got home? When Dad got home? I would keep my eyes fixed on the road approaching the car park to see if I could spot her driving along in her red Mini. I always remember that I could tell from a good distance whether or not she had been drinking, not by the way she drove the car, but by the look in her eye. Even from 100 yards or more, if she had a certain look in her eye then she had been drinking. She wasn't necessarily drunk, but she had been drinking, and I could tell instantly. And I knew what it would lead to later on.

If she had been drinking, as she pulled the car up to let us get in, I would be full of both fear and anger towards her. As soon as the car door opened, the smell would hit me: a mixture of cigarettes, alcohol and the perfume used to disguise it. I would always sit in the front seat so that I could keep an eye on things. She had a tendency to take her eyes off the road and hands off the wheel as she attempted to light another cigarette.

There was always plenty of schoolboy chatter in the car – a tactic I would use so that she wouldn't talk, and so that my friend Stephen wouldn't realise that she had been drinking. When she did say something it was often funny, and Stephen seemed to find her very entertaining.

When we eventually got to Stephen's house, he would run up the driveway, often to be met by his mother on the doorstep. I wanted so desperately to go with him. I knew the chaos that lay ahead when we got home. I wanted his mum to be my mum. In fact, I just wanted a 'normal mum'.

Thankfully my mum got sober when I turned 12 and she became the 'normal mum' I had so longed for. She has been in recovery for the last 30 plus years, thanks to her ongoing commitment to AA. She is a wonderful woman who I respect greatly and love dearly!

The son of a mother-in-recovery recounts a life-changing winter's night.

Open Window

One winter's night when I was about 13 or 14 years old I was awoken from a deep sleep by the voice of my father shouting. 'What are you doing? It's freezing, get back in here . . . Mary, Mary!' It was coming from my parent's bedroom, which was directly opposite mine. It wasn't unusual to hear their raised voices at night, but this time there was a different tone in my father's voice. He sounded both scared and angry all at once. I looked at my bedside clock – it was just after 3 a.m.

I jumped out of bed and ran into their room. There, I found my dad, standing in his pyjamas beside an open window. My mum had climbed through it, wearing just her nightie, and was gone. My dad frantically pulled on some clothes and ran out into the garden, and then onto the road looking for her, but she had disappeared into the cold night. The police were called; they came along with some relatives. I was told to go back to bed which I eventually did, but I couldn't sleep. Mum was gone! I didn't understand why as she had seemed so much better since she stopped drinking the year before (after a three month stay in hospital). What was going on? Why had she disappeared in the middle of the night?

The next morning, everybody kept saying to me that everything would be alright, that mum would come back or be found and that she would be ok. The police, my family and friends were all out looking for her. It was one of the longest days of my life. Every time the phone rang I jumped. Had they found her? Was she alright? Was she coming home? Was she dead?

At about 6 p.m. that evening, she was found by the police wandering in a daze on the beach. She was covered in sand and had scratches and bruising to her face and body. It turned out that she had walked up a hill in the pitch darkness, had somehow made her way down to the beach and had obviously fallen a few times. When she was brought home to get cleaned up, I was overwhelmingly relieved to see her, but also shocked and frightened to see the state she was in. She looked like a wild animal.

Having gone into recovery from alcohol addiction the year before, my mum bravely decided that she wanted to get totally clean. This meant addressing her dependency on prescription drugs which had built up over the years. She had tried to do it on her own and had totally underestimated both the physical and psychological effects of withdrawal. She admits to this day that it very nearly killed her.

With a lot of determination and help my mum got herself totally clean and has been in recovery for over 35 years. She uses her own experiences to help other people going through similar problems with alcohol and prescription drugs. I am very proud of her and love her very much.

M x

An eight-year-old girl expresses her feelings to her uncle in addiction.

Dear Uncle

I hope you are well now? But why did you upset my mammy?

It scared me when I didn't know what was going on. If Mum or Granny got a call saying that something happened to you, they would be crying afterwards. It was a terrible feeling.

You are fine one time and next you're back to your terrible self. You are better, but every time I see you I wonder, 'Will you be like this forever, or will you go back to your same old self?'

To know there was nothing I could do, it was terrible. Everybody tried everything they could do for you. We let you stay in our house but still you did it again and you got taken away in an ambulance. It was really scary.

Why did you do that to your family? Why did you do that to yourself? You do not have to have drink to enjoy life.

Love from your niece

A woman tells her friend how his addiction tested their relationship and how his recovery is mending it.

Dear Friend

When we first met I thought all my birthdays had come together. We had such craic. You had such a happy way about you – I loved your childlike giddiness and ridiculous sense of humour. You were a bit older than me but we had lots in common. It was lovely getting to know each other.

You were a people person; it was part of your job really. You had a brilliant job that really mattered. Your family are lovely, you couldn't have come from a more loving and supportive family. For the life of me I couldn't understand why you had any demons, but you did.

When we met, you had been off the drink for a few months but had recently slipped back. You thought you could still have a few and control it. I had no clue at this stage; it hadn't even dawned on me. But then you'd turn up drunk for dates when it was way too early to be drinking or be that tipsy. I noticed you'd be messier than me at the end of a night. Soon I'd want to go home earlier but you'd always want to go on later. I didn't necessarily want to go home early – I just didn't want you to have anymore drink. Weird that I hadn't twigged there was a problem, but obviously I did on some level.

Drinking is so acceptable in Ireland, I looked like the killjoy girlfriend. We would fight; it was embarrassing because I even screamed and cried at you in front of our friends once. Sure, everybody drank. That's just what we did, in college and afterwards. I was outing you and you were so good at hiding it all. None of your family knew. At my family get-togethers we left early. My family and friends couldn't understand it when we broke up. They thought I was mad. The only people I ever told about your drinking problem were my dad and my boss.

We got closer again and you would tell me more, but only when you were wasted – you knew you had a problem. You'd been fighting it for ten years before you met me. Then you'd sober up and go straight back to denial. It was frustrating; I wanted to help but only realised much later that I couldn't. I began to realise there was this crazy battle going on in your head and I had just landed right in the middle of something I had no comprehension of. This was a scary place. But I wanted to help you; I wasn't running.

My flatmate didn't like you. He thought I was mad and he didn't even know the half of it. I wouldn't hear of it so he shut up and didn't interfere.

But you never lost your temper, a gentle soul to the core even when you were in an awful mess. In fact, I would get so angry that I was probably the scarier of the two of us. You were so good at hiding the drinking, but it steadily got worse. You'd stop for a bit and then go back and get worse again. I'd get calls at work that made my face go white. I'd be physically sick with the worry. You would be in a pub in the middle of nowhere, where no one would recognise you. You travelled with work so you got away with it and the girls at work loved you and covered for you. You always managed to deliver; I'm still not sure how you did that. Once you sobered up, you would be kicking yourself that you had phoned me, not because I was upset but because I was onto you again. I wouldn't let up talking about it, and then I would lull myself into a false sense of security thinking that everything would be grand now again.

Then you had an accident. I came to get you; you could have killed yourself. You were all bloodied up. You told me later that you even scared yourself then; you knew it was getting worse. By this stage, I had a constant headache, and I couldn't sleep much with the worry. So many times I wanted to ring your brother, but you would die if your family found out, and I wouldn't ring your parents. They were so gentle; I would never do that. So I told my dad. He didn't judge you; he knew you were lovely too. He never asked any questions, or told anyone else. He let me make up my own mind, but I wasn't coping with the stress. I felt alone with this. I felt guilty that I didn't stay, that I couldn't cope. I felt weak and selfish.

Anyway, things have worked out for you. Very soon after, you rang me to tell me you were in recovery. I knew you were facing your biggest fears – you had told your family and they helped you get the help you needed. When I visited you, it was fine. You wanted your best friends to visit and I was happy to be included as one of them, and you weren't keeping it such a big secret anymore.

That is nine years ago now; you don't drink at all

anymore. We are still friends; every time I meet you I see a change – you are more confident in yourself and more relaxed. I admire you so much. You went on a journey of self-discovery, and you do all the things you are so talented at again.

I am so glad we are friends. You are one of the softest, kindest people I know.

Anonymous

We Laughed, We Cried . . .

So there they were, five of the most beautiful boys from the estate, knocking at *my* door ☺ . . .

'What do you mean my da is blocking yer goal post? Move him yourself,' and I slammed the door ☹ . . .

Detachment

'He who would be serene and pure needs but one thing, detachment.'

Meister Eckhart

In addiction, the concept of 'detaching' provides a tool for recovery, whether it's detaching from the addiction itself or the addictive behaviour of a loved one.

There is a saying in addiction recovery that goes 'we are only as sick as our secrets'. The premise behind this saying is that our secrets will keep our addiction alive and kicking. Many turn to addiction as a way to suppress emotions or traumatic events that were never dealt with in a healthy, appropriate manner. The problem that occurs after someone has been caught in the grip of drug, alcohol, food, or gambling abuse for a long time is that they know of no other way to deal with their problems. After years of being dependent on a substance or a behaviour, how is someone going to be able to retrain themselves to cope with their past issues in a healthy manner without turning to chemical or behavioural dependency?

Most people who struggle with alcohol and drug addiction may have numerous failed attempts to stop their abuse on their own. Detaching from addiction is one of the first steps towards recovery. Detaching and letting go is a practice in surrender, a very useful life-improving practice to cultivate. Letting go of addiction can pull us back into a quality of life that we didn't even realise we had lost.

Detaching with love is a very important therapeutic goal for family members in recovery. Detachment, in an addiction context, means letting go of efforts to control or take responsibility for the person in addiction. We must understand that detaching with love does not mean to 'walk away' or 'leave' the person we are concerned about. It means caring enough about our loved one to allow them to learn from their mistakes, and letting them take responsibility for their own behaviour.

Addiction not only has a typical progression for our loved one, there is a similar progression for family members as well. As addiction progresses, our loved one becomes more and more disabled by their addiction. During this progression, a family member can feel compelled to take on an increasing amount of our loved one's roles and responsibilities. They often take on the job of 'minding' the adult addict. The person in addiction feels compelled to continue to use the substance in the face of negative consequences. As this happens, the family member can be similarly 'compelled'. They observe their loved one losing control over his or her life, and feel that they have to do everything they can to prevent this from happening, or to fix it. This compulsion to 'take control' is a typical part of the family dynamics of addiction.

Often the family member can get stuck in negative patterns when they try to find ways to detach from their loved one in addiction, and this can cause many problems. If they have tried everything and their loved one just does not want to end their addiction, there are tools that they can learn. Detaching with love for the family member means that they can live a healthy life, and their loved one might then see that they need to change and may seek help.

Detaching with love does not have to involve anger. It does not involve a withdrawal of love or support. It does not involve a hopeless or desperate acceptance of the unacceptable. Detachment with love is about emotionally, mentally and sometimes physically letting go of unhealthy entanglements. Family members do not cause their loved one's addiction, nor can they control or cure addiction. What family members can do is find support, set boundaries, detach with love, and eventually discover how to enjoy life, whether their loved one finds recovery or not.

Frances

Rachael Keogh, author of 'Dying to Survive', looks back on the way in which her addiction impacted on her family.

Addiction, by its very nature, is a disease which rots humans to their core with selfishness and blinds them to any damage that they might be doing to themselves or their loved ones.

I know this because I am one of those people. I am an addict who has an illness that lies to me. It tells me that I haven't got an illness and that I'm not the problem. It tells me that everyone else is the problem and if only everyone would leave me alone then I would be perfectly happy and the world would be a wonderful place.

The funny thing is that at the end of my drug use, when I finally was left alone, I painfully realised the truth. That it wasn't my family or the world who needed help – it was me. It amazes me to think of the amount of rock bottoms and near-death experiences that I had to endure before I came to this awakening.

It took my family 14 years before they took a step back from me. God love them. I honestly don't know how they put up with me. Especially my grandmother. She was the one who reared me and she witnessed it all first-hand. There was my grandparents; my mother, who gave birth to me when she was 15 and was more like my sister; and then there was my two aunties and my two uncles. They watched me go from being a happy-go-lucky child who loved school and who had everything to live for, to being someone who rip-roared my way through their lives and anyone else who came close to me. Taking all that I could just to make myself feel good. My family were left as baffled as me.

They were shocked to find out that I was taking drugs. Sure, I was only 12 years old. At a time when I should have been swapping fancy paper and listening to Kylie Minogue, I was hanging around the blocks in Ballymun smoking hash, drinking alcohol and taking acid. How did that happen? That's the thing about addiction: it sneaks up behind you and gets you in its grip when you're not looking. And no one ever thinks that it will happen to them. I certainly didn't. I was way too clever for the likes of that. I would never be anything like them junkies who hang around the shops. The state of them. I was only having a bit of fun and I could stop whenever I wanted to. I just didn't want to, that was all. At least that's what I told myself.

My family knew very little about addiction and they thought that I was going through some form of adolescent phase that I would surely grow out of. Little did they know that they would end up living like prisoners in their own home. Having to lock every room in the house because I was fleecing them blind to feed my habit. Little did my grandmother know that she would spend years visiting me in Mountjoy Women's Prison. Little did they know that they would have to send me halfway around the world in a bid to get me help. Always wondering whether or not they were doing the right thing. The alternative being that I would overdose and die. Then, the devastating blow of relapse after relapse. The sleepless nights, the emotional turmoil and despair as they waited to get that call to say that I had been found in some ditch. Little did they know that they would have to watch on helplessly as my addiction progressed like a cancer to the point where I was self-mutilating and sticking needles into the open wounds on my arms that were the result of chronic heroin abuse.

Did I realise the effect that my addiction was having on my family? To be honest, not for one second. Not because I was a bad person or morally incompetent, but because I was very sick and I couldn't possibly think of anyone but myself. Deep down, I genuinely wanted to do the right thing by my family and myself. How many times had I said, 'I promise I will stop, I'll never do it again'? And I would mean every word. Only to find myself using again. My willpower was insufficient in the light of my addiction. My hands were tied behind my back and I had completely lost the power of choice.

Eventually my family realised that I had gone well beyond the stage of being reached or saved. My mother and my brother moved to a different country to start a new life. And the rest of my family just left me alone. I can honestly say that this proved to be my saving grace. I no longer had my family to cushion my fall. I could no longer blame them for my behaviour. I was 26 years of age and I was dying. That was the loneliest time of my life. It was at that point that I had no one to turn to but God. And I wasn't really on speaking terms with Him either. But I had two options: to die a drug addict or to fight for my life.

Somewhere in all of that I found the strength to become drug-free. I am now almost five years in recovery. I have a beautiful baby boy who has created so much healing between myself and my family. Through my son, I get to show my family that I have changed. It is only in the past couple of years that I have really seen how my addiction impacted my family. I realise now that it was possibly worse for them than it was for me. At least I was sedated in it all. They had nothing to block the pain. But they loved me and supported me nonetheless. I went as low as a person can go with my addiction and I know in my heart that without my family, I would be dead. But if they had continued to enable me, I would have died anyway. Them letting me go was the most loving thing that they ever could have done for me and for themselves.

Rachael Keogh

In a letter to her children, a mother describes her experience of their father's addiction to alcohol.

This letter is to my four lovely children and to the fifth who is waiting for us in heaven.

I married your dad thinking that love would see us through, but unfortunately, on too many occasions, alcohol was stronger than love. I struggled for years to understand how alcohol could change your dad from a good guy to a completely uncaring individual. Even when he was not drinking, his mood could change from passive to volatile in a split second if things were not going his way. At times, I thought it was just me being too fussy, but as the years progressed I realised that living in fear of your dad was causing me a lot of stress. I also felt guilty because I was teaching you all that to live in fear was acceptable, and that it was ok for alcohol to dictate our lives. I was also teaching you not to confront problems and to ignore the subtle control of your dad's moods. We were on a rollercoaster, going from great times to absolute misery, without realising that living like this was abnormal.

I was searching for someone to understand what I was going through, searching for support and guidance. I had been making crazy decisions, like putting your dad out of the house only to take him back a few days later in the hope that he would learn that we could never depend on him when he was drinking. As you all know, this only served to create more instability and upset, and for that I am truly sorry. My problem was that I did not realise that, in order for things to get better, I had to take control of my life, and not allow alcohol and everything associated with it to dictate our lives. You are my priority and I am so lucky to have such lovely, vibrant children.

A dear friend, who the four of you know well, recommended an excellent counsellor, who, in turn, suggested that I might find support in The RISE Foundation. I didn't know what to expect as I had not heard of this organisation but I knew I could not carry on the way things were going. Thank God for his recommendation because at last I had found other people whose families were all affected by addiction. The support of the counsellor and fellow group members is also very comforting and I have made dear friends for life whom I hope to introduce to you all some day.

Thanks to them, I have found a safe place to work on myself and rebuild my confidence. Sometimes it's a struggle to stay strong and detach from your dad. He is a good man and I love him, but I have learned that I can't change him. It is up to him to admit what his problems are, and if that ever happens, I will support him and offer him the help he needs. He is your dad and I know you all love him to pieces.

I want you to be aware that, because alcohol addiction is in our family, there is a possibility that at least one of you could have problems with it. All I can say to you is to please be aware of this and if you feel at all that alcohol is becoming a problem, leave it behind. Look at all the pain it has caused us; you don't need this in your lives.

The RISE Foundation has been a Godsend to me. I would still be on that crazy rollercoaster if it were not for them. I realise that I will continue to need support in order to stay strong, so if I am cranky at times, please try and understand that it's because I am struggling to recover from the effects of alcohol on our lives.

That's about all for now, gang. I hope this letter will give you some insight into how I have been feeling for the past number of years. Thanks for being a great bunch to have around (even if we all do drive each other crazy at times). Life can only get better for us now.

Love you all to pieces,
Mam xxOO

A woman expresses how the concern of a neighbour made her realise that she didn't need to deal with her problems alone.

'Mammy, why did you throw Daddy out?'

'No, love, I didn't. It's just sometimes Mammys and Daddys split up, they need a break.'

'But Daddy told me you did.'

The tears were waiting to burst through my eyes, and it hurt me to try and hold them in. But when he ran off into school, all the emotions came out: anger, hurt, sadness, confusion. When I finally pulled myself together, I couldn't dial the numbers fast enough. 'How could you, you selfish pig? Putting all the blame on me!'

This went on for months – the games, the threats, the lies, the jealousy, the arguments. But the absolute worst was how you were abusing our son emotionally. My little boy would cry at night because you told him over the phone that you were lonely. You told him that I wouldn't let you come home. You told him that I stopped you from bringing him out one week when you knew damn well that I couldn't let him go with you because you were drunk.

Our little boy had to attend a special group in school to help him deal with our separation. Thank God our little girl was too young to understand what was going on.

He would get angry with me, throwing tantrums, and I even caught him hitting his little sister. He didn't ask for this, and he was too young to understand how to handle it.

You were great when you were sober and his days out with you consisted of trips to McDonalds and Smyth's Toys, and being spoiled rotten by his adoring grandparents, but I had to do all the normal day-to-day stuff. School runs, football practice, sickness, boldness and punishing him when he was naughty. I didn't always have the time to sit and listen to his every word, so no wonder he saw me as the baddie – I would too!

My patience was wearing thin. I sometimes found myself shouting at him and then I felt so guilty when he said, 'Mammy, you're scaring me!'.

One day I'd just had enough. Our son had slapped me across the face and I just didn't have the strength to even open the bundle of bills that lay sitting on the table. I know now that this was a very low point for me, a kind of breakdown. I was so tired of surviving – living hand-to-mouth, running from work to the school, cleaning and trying to juggle everything that I just cracked. As the children were sleeping I got it into my head that we would all be better off dead.

I was actually running through ideas in my head trying to figure out how I could do it, when suddenly I just started screaming. I was so scared of myself that I ran out onto our street. I just had to get out of the house. Luckily my neighbour was returning from work when she saw me, hysterical, in the garden. She thought that something had happened to the baby.

When she got me back into the house and made me a cup of tea, it all came rushing out – through the sobs, snots, and tears I told her absolutely everything. She hugged me like a mother and told me about a group of women who met each week in my area – she told me they could help. She told me things that night that I never knew about her. All these years we had lived in the same neighbourhood but we were oblivious to each other's stories.

Going along to the women's group has saved my life and the lives of my children. I have received so much advice and support, and through them have also been directed to other agencies who can help with some of the other problems, like MABs and the Legal Centre.

I did a parenting course in my community which has helped me with our little son, and now I am in college studying Community and Family Support. I am much happier in myself than ever before. There are still some problems but I know I am not alone – I get through each day with a lot of support from my new friends around me.

A recovering alcoholic ponders his new social options since giving up the drink.

What's Wrong with Me?

Getting used to the new me is not easy at all
I'm sitting here wondering who could I call
Well there's James, me ol' mate, but sure it's Friday at
  nine
So he'll be in some fancy restaurant on his second
  bottle of wine
With some of the gang from the job there's no doubt
And Jimmy my other mate's in Gibney's on the stout
My girlfriend's out with her happy bunch
'Cause they were having their Christmas late boozy
  lunch

I'm miserable and lonely, it's the season of Cheer
Jaysus, what I would give for a cold pint of beer
I can't let everyone down again, I'm trying my best
What's wrong with me that I ended up in this mess?

If I make it through Christmas sure then it'll be BBQ
  time
The lads with their cold beers and the girls on the
  wine
Sure weddings, funerals, christenings and all
It wouldn't be an Irish celebration without alcohol

21sts, communions, party excuses galore
They're only occasions so we can drink more
I've too many triggers, they're all around me
I can't enjoy the match with a nice cup of tea

I feel like a weirdo and I must look like one too
When everyone's out just having a few
With me one leads to two, three, four and more
And then it's not over until I hit the floor

I'm a right lonely freak, I wish someone would call
I should be able to go out on a Friday evening
Sure I'm a young man after all!

We Laughed, We Cried . . .

'Wasn't it an awful pity that our ol' fella couldn't have been addicted to his kids? Could have made life a lot easier . . . '

Forgiveness

'Holding on to anger, resentment and hurt only gives you tense muscles, a headache and a sore jaw from clenching your teeth. Forgiveness gives you back the laughter and the lightness in your life.'

Joan Lunden

One key element that will further progress in addiction recovery is forgiveness. We must forgive ourselves. It may be difficult to let go of the guilt that is carried as a result of years of irresponsibility. There is a lot of hurt caused by addiction, which may result in physical, emotional, psychological or financial damage to a loved one. Partners, children, parents, siblings, and friends can all be devastated by a loved one's addictive behaviour. When we step into recovery these past actions can leave us feeling ashamed and guilty and, for some, can result in relapse.

Feeling guilty should not be confused with taking responsibility for the past. Taking responsibility means that we actively address the consequences of our actions in whatever way we can, in particular by changing our behaviour patterns, which means abstaining from the addictive substance or behaviour. Taking responsibility also includes moving on by making amends with the people we have hurt in our lives and making sure that we do not repeat any old behaviours. It means letting go of any grudges or resentments that we may be harbouring over certain things that were said, or actions taken that we believe were thoughtless, cruel, unjust, or just plain unfair. Resentment can be the number one offender when it comes to addiction relapse; holding onto resentment can stall the recovery process.

The feelings that surround the family members of a loved one in addiction can range from sadness to despair, anger to frustration. We may feel a sense of confusion and perhaps even devastation. We may ask, 'How and where do I start on the road to process all this grief?' We may feel, 'If I start to cry, I won't be able to stop' or 'My heart is permanently broken'. The reality is that it is possible to get the support we need to help process the grief we are feeling. Our tears, rage, and hurt come to an end when we allow ourselves to express them. We may feel sad or enraged, from time to time, but we will not be 'THERE' permanently. Our hearts can be mended if we allow them to be healed properly.

Unprocessed feelings go inward, creating unhealthy patterns, anxiety, depression, self-doubt, rage, and ultimately a loss of a sense of self or a feeling of numbness. Processing feelings with someone who has the ability to listen will help to start the release process that we need for our own recovery. Forgiveness can be difficult when it comes to living with someone in addiction for a long time, as sometimes hurt from the past seem to block our way into the future. It is important for the family member to learn how to let go and forgive in order to begin their own recovery. Forgiveness can be a gift to ourselves. As mentioned earlier, holding on to resentment is not good. Resentment is like drinking poison and expecting the other person to die – it is self-destructive.

Moving forward in our recovery, whether we are in

recovery from addiction or a family member, means we need a clean slate. This is required for true progress, and the way we can achieve that clean slate is through forgiveness.

Frances

*A father of a son in addiction
describes the process of recovery.*

Before I first came to my support group I felt isolated, and I felt that my problems set me apart from everyone else. I lived in a constant state of fear, guilt and shame. I felt everyone knew what my child was doing and blamed me. After all, if I was a good 'enough parent', he would not be involved with drugs and the behaviour that went with it.

I felt angry most of the time at so many people, places and things but mainly at myself. How could I not have known what was happening? People: if he wasn't with Johnny or Jim he wouldn't be using. Places: that lane in Togher, why didn't the police move the dealers on? Things: my son – how did he do these things to me? I took his using and behaviour personally – after all, if he loved me, he wouldn't use and behave as he did. I found I was angry and irritable all the time. My behaviour was becoming as bad as the addict's. I was now slamming doors, shouting and name-calling, not the best way to handle a difficult situation.

Only another parent can know the pain that watching a child in addiction brings. The dashed hopes and sense of loss of what might have been. Guilt added to the pain. I was watching him slowly kill himself. Why wasn't he working or in third-level education? He had been a very bright lad with a good work ethic. We celebrated his twenty-first birthday without him – that was such a sad day for me. We went for a meal with my family without the birthday boy – he was too stoned. The pain of having my son disrespect me, my home, neighbours, other family members and the police while under the influence was often unbearable. I found myself thinking at times that he would be better off dead, and at times wishing I was, but that wasn't an option as who would look after him if I was gone?

I became obsessed with needing to know where he was, what he was doing; searching his room, his phone, clothes; waiting up for him to come in, not being able to sleep until he did. He was often unable to sleep because he would be high and keep everyone awake.

I neglected myself, my relationships, my work, my friends and social life. The few times we got a break, there was always a phone call and a crisis. I resented my son and other parents whose kids had no problems. I lived on false hopes, promises and disappointments. I couldn't enjoy the good moments as there was always a crisis waiting for me, tomorrow, next week.

I had little boundaries in my home. They were never respected. This made me feel used and worthless. I was made to feel guilty for trying to set rules in the house. The addict threatened to move out if he couldn't drink or use in his room. That scared me. How could I control him if he moved out? I tried letting him use at home so that it would be safer. That was a huge mistake.

My support group has offered me a safe haven. Our meetings start with tea and, if we are lucky, some nice cakes. When I sit on my chair I feel the tension beginning to ease. It is such a relief to be with people who had or have similar problems and experiences. I no longer feel isolated and alone. I am beginning to build my self-esteem as I am accepted as I am and don't feel judged. Although I am unique, my situation is so similar to others' at the group, at times it feels we are living with the same children.

I learned I didn't cause the addiction; I can't control it and I can't cure it. I am letting go of the guilt and shame and, with it, huge pain and sadness. The group helps me to see that I did the best that I could at the time.

It is great identifying with others in the group. Listening to others sharing is often more healing than sharing myself. I sometimes can see myself as I was which gives me hope that I am changing for the better. I see myself as I am now and how I am dealing with things differently.

I have learned the importance of boundaries and how to put them in place. I know I can only change myself and not my son. I am learning different ways to communicate and better ways of dealing with conflicts and disagreements. I let a lot of things go over my head now, realising it is not worth the energy trying to fight some battles. I am letting go of the need to control. It's not gone yet but I am getting better.

I have learned the importance of detachment and am getting better at it. I have a long way to go yet. I am learning not to have expectations as they only lead to disappointment and hurt if they are not realised. I am trying to focus more on myself to forgive myself and let go of the guilt and shame. I am healing the hurt.

With the help of our wonderful facilitator, I am learning

more about my son's addiction, its affects on him and us as a family. I realise his addiction is an illness and his behaviour is not a personal attack on me. It doesn't mean he loves me any less but that the addiction is stronger. I am giving him the dignity to make his own choices and mistakes.

I am learning about the power and necessity of living for now, and how important it is to keep the things in the day. This is so hard, because I constantly project. I can see how being obsessed only serves to drive me, and all around me, insane. I am finding it easier to reach out for help and I am able to offer help. I am learning self-acceptance, self-esteem, tolerance, trust and honesty.

My son is in recovery for now. I didn't expect to experience such huge sadness and grief when he found recovery. I thought all my problems would be over. Thanks to the members of our group, I am able to deal with it and express it in a safe way and place. I wasn't involved in my son's recovery process as much as I would have liked. I feel it is important for treatment services to include family members in the process as addiction affects the whole family, not just the drug user. The healing power that I have found through sharing our experiences, pain, joy, and wisdom cannot be measured. The members of my support group are a unique set of people on a painful, but worthwhile, journey together.

Our recovery can only strengthen ourselves, our families and our loved ones in addiction. Thanks to all who have made this happen. The group is a lifeline for me and many other parents that attend it. Long may our group continue.

A woman writes to her husband about
the shocking revelation of his gambling addiction,
and the extent of their debts.

I'm stronger today because of the support I have received from my peer group, but this wasn't always the case.

When I married you, I thought I was the luckiest woman in the world. It was a fabulous day, everyone was so happy. We were childhood sweethearts; we shared the same friends, and our families were very close – like one. Both of our families were well-respected in our community, all local business people. You worked very hard, so much so that your father trusted you to take over the running of the family business.

I still can't believe, to this day, the events that have taken place over the last three years.

So there we are all are in the family portrait taken at our only daughter's wedding, the smiles beaming on our faces. You're so proud – you had cried that morning as she walked down the stairs and took your arm; you cried as you proudly walked her up the aisle. You cried too the morning she was born as you told me how proud you were of me. After five beautiful sons we were delighted to be blessed with such a beautiful baby girl.

So now she was getting married. It was a fantastic day, the sun was shining and everything went so well. The lovely speeches and all the joking about. It was like our own wedding. We felt so, so lucky to be all there together, with her five brothers standing tall beside her. Frank, her new husband, is a fine young man; we couldn't have picked a nicer person ourselves.

So it came as a huge surprise and shock to me to get that call when they arrived back from their honeymoon. They had arrived in late the night before so I was dying to see them that Sunday morning.

'Mam,' she said when I answered the phone, and I knew immediately from the tone of her voice that something was wrong. 'Mam, I need to speak to you. Are you there alone? Can I come over?'

Can she come over? What a silly thing to say!

I saw the hurt in her eyes, she couldn't hide the hurt. I immediately thought it was her husband, wondered what had he done.

'What's wrong, love?' I asked. 'Please tell me.'

'Daddy has been lying.'

'What?' I could not believe my ears.

She told me everything. About how you had borrowed money from her. How you had made her get a loan from the bank to lend you money to pay for her wedding. I thought we had paid for her wedding – I was in total shock. And how you had borrowed money from our son-in-law's family too – thirty grand to be exact – some months before. I heard all about the excuses, the cash flow problems, that he was waiting on a cheque etc. She had only found out about that because on honeymoon she had decided to tell her husband about the bank loan, even though you had told her not to tell anyone. She didn't want to enter into marriage with secrets. But then he told her about the loan from his father and about how you had not paid it back and that his father was worried about your 'gambling problem'.

Our poor child must have felt so humiliated, ashamed and scared. Of course, her husband didn't mean to hurt her but she was devastated. He had to call his father on the phone to speak to her, to console her, to reassure her that this was not her fault. His dad was annoyed with him for telling her – and on their honeymoon of all times – but he told them to try and enjoy what was left of their honeymoon and that he would have a meeting with them on their return.

And so began the chaos and despair – the confusion, the confrontation, the big family meeting. The checking of paperwork, and meetings with our accountants, bank manager and people you owed money to. The shame, the embarrassment, the fear of becoming homeless. Thank God for the support and understanding of our new in-laws. True to his word, Frank's father put a plan together. It was very helpful to have his accountancy experience to guide us through the web of problems.

Things were really, really bad. When the reality of our situation had set in, we realised we were hundreds of thousands of euro in debt. We had to remortgage our home. Eventually, while in treatment, you had to write down a list of the people you owed money to and I cried when I saw some of our closest friends on the list. The shock almost killed me. I never saw this coming – you were an amazing husband, a wonderful, loving father. I trusted you with my life. You didn't drink or smoke, you never had. I ran the home, and you ran the business and all the finances. I was busy with the kids and then the grandkids; sure I had no reason to doubt you. I know you never planned for it to get that bad.

I have received great support from my family support group and through counselling. I have learned to forgive you, and my faith in God has brought me through this. I am grateful to God that you survived your suicide attempt but I was very angry with you that you were prepared to check out and leave me to pick up the pieces alone.

But I'm not alone. I still have our beautiful children and grandchildren – the little ones are innocent and unaware, I'm also grateful for that. They can still grow up with a grandfather who adores them and not have to live with the stigma and shame that suicide brings to so many families.

Ok, my pride has been dented but although we have lost the business, we still have good friends who have stood by us. We don't have much, but we were able to pay back the money we owed.

I understand that our problems did not just happen overnight and that there were other factors involved. This horrible recession and the downturn in the business had just escalated these problems. I know how heartbreaking it was for you to walk away from the business, your father's business. To lose that was terrible, but we had a lot more to lose if we didn't pay people back: our respectability as good, honest people.

So we lost a lot but there was no point in sitting, worrying, when the phone rang or a knock came to the door. At least this way we can still hold our heads up high and enjoy what is left of our lives with our beautiful family. Some poor unfortunates don't get that chance!

A woman describes to her husband the fallout from his sex addiction.

Dear Husband

So now I'm the lunatic who can't stop checking for clues. I check your text messages, your Facebook profile, the phone bills and your pockets. I can't go on like this much longer. I know I'm out of control – it's making me sick. I'm constantly worrying about when the next big humiliating episode is going to kick off. Will it be someone I know this time?

How could I have been so stupid so as not to have noticed what you were doing? Ok so I've changed since you met me, and after two pregnancies I don't feel so attractive anymore, but I naively thought we were happy, that you were happy. Two healthy children, a lovely home, and, up until ten months ago, a very happy life. We had a future planned together. I trusted you. I know it's hard in the entertainment business, with you away a lot and girls throwing themselves at you but I honestly thought that you were strong. We had dreams, and I wanted you to have your dreams as much as I wanted to have my own. I was content to stay at home with our family keeping everything going here.

So when you admitted in front of the marriage counsellor that you have had over 60 sexual encounters, and you couldn't even be sure exactly how many took place during our relationship, I felt physically sick. The humiliation, the embarrassment, and the hurt were unbearable.

I had heard stories about men who constantly cheated on their wives. It had happened to some of our closest friends. You had even discussed their marital problems with me over dinner and on nights out, but you always reassured me that you were not like that, that you were not silly enough to throw away your perfect family life, when you have steak at home and all that crap!

The pain soon turned to anger. I had never asked for much. I wasn't greedy but you obviously were. You had not only lied but had put both of our lives in danger multiple times.

The counsellor recommended that I go to a special clinic to get tested for STDs. It was the worst day of my life. I felt cheap and dirty. When the nurse asked me the required questions I started to sob, and that poor nurse, she was so kind. I had to tell her the truth; I did not want her to think that I was some slut who was stupid enough not to use protection.

This stranger was the first person that I had told since you broke the news. She listened while the whole story came out. She was very understanding. It was she who told me about the support group and the meetings that helped her through a similar situation.

I have changed and I don't know if I will ever be able to return to the woman I once was. I thought I was enough for you. I thought our relationship, our home, our life together was built on trust and love, but it was full of illusions.

So you're a sex addict in recovery, with all the promises

in the world to change. I'm also in recovery, taking it one day at a time, but I don't know if I will ever fully recover.

At weddings and gatherings with our friends and family, I used to love to watch you mingle and laugh out loud. I felt so proud to be by your side; I was married to a wonderfully sociable man. It brought a smile to my face when you'd laugh and tell stories that made the party. But lately I dread these social occasions. I scan the room to see if I can notice anything out of the ordinary, signs to say that you have been with one of the gorgeous girls in our company who have youth on their side.

So now I bounce between being a mother of two gorgeous, innocent children and attending our counselling sessions, and meeting my 'new friends' at the support group. It helps to be able to offload some of the crap feelings and know that I am not being judged, that I'm not alone. But I can't help feeling that I am just as bad as you now. I have become part of the lies and deceit, the illusion. I'm a liar, a cheat to our friends and family who think that everything is great in our lives. The lovely house, the X5, the good school our children attend, the jewellery, the lifestyle – it all means nothing now.

Dear Friend

You went into Rehab wanting to Die and left wanting to
Live.

To me that says it all . . .

We Laughed, We Cried . . .

'It wasn't easy trying to hide the ol' fella lying drunk, again, on the hall floor while we tried to rob the money out of his pockets to pay the pizza delivery man.'

We Laughed, We Cried . . .

'I was thinking about something to write regarding my recovery, and it dawned on me that I was thinking . . . Ma, you would say that was progress!

True Potential

'Most of the shadows of this life are caused by our
standing in our own sunshine.'

Ralph Waldo Emerson

This quote is so true. Addiction can get in the way of our own true potential. It can stop us from doing great things within our grasp. It can take away all that is good in our lives. It can rob us of family, dignity, confidence, self-respect, positive healthy relationships with those we love, our power and eventually even our lives. Addiction affects the way we think and feel, and how we live our lives. It will stunt our growth process. It keeps us from becoming the whole and complete people that we can be. True potential is stifled. In addiction we miss out on so much in life.

It is exactly the same for family members or concerned persons: watching someone you love and care for destroying their life with alcohol, drugs, gambling, or food can be soul-destroying. You may feel worn out, angry, sad, lost and powerless. The feeling of constant preoccupation with where your loved one is and if they are safe can be exhausting. You may feel angry. The loss of trust has far-reaching emotional and psychological effects that can last a lifetime. Children who grow up with parents in addiction often feel they can never trust anyone. As a family member or concerned person, you, just like your loved one in addiction, can end up feeling robbed of your dignity, confidence, self respect, positive healthy relationships with those you love and in some cases, even life. The emotional impact of these feelings will get in the way of your true potential.

That is why recovery for both parties can be life-changing, for the person in addiction and the family member or concerned person. It is vitally important to seek help to come to this awareness. It may not be an easy journey – there may be a few mountains to climb – but accepting powerlessness will lead to changes in your understanding, your attitudes, and your behaviours. In time you will experience a new kind of freedom.

How can we reconnect with our true potential?

We can start by breaking the silence, talking to someone we feel safe with. Verbally processing issues can help our awareness of them, and pave the road towards resolving them. Listen to your emotions. Emotions are the nerves to the soul. Emotions may be scary and unfamiliar at first, as we have covered them with a substance or a behaviour, or, for family members, a preoccupation with our loved one in addiction for so long. Our emotions are essential in changing our lives. They will tell us when our lives are off-course. We must listen to them. If we are having negative emotions, we must look at them as a signal that change is needed.

Mediation can help us by grounding us, and allowing us to remember the abilities and strengths we possess to overcome painful and negative emotions.

We as human beings, regardless of race, sex or spiritual belief, have the incredible capacity to accomplish far beyond what we think our limits are. We have unbelievable strength and courage, we only have to tap into it.

Frances

A woman describes how it feels to truly open her eyes to the possibility of starting anew.

I Can See

Going round in circles is ok, it happens so quickly when you lose sight. Even when the most beautiful 'everything' you believed in and wanted all your life is happening right before your very eyes – you can lose sight.

The mind and the world around you, the people, the things we can say and do to one another can twist and turn your insides out.

It's about a moment like this, when the world reminds you in the smallest of ways how great you are, how you've always been. How true love is, and hope. And when you lose heart just open your eyes again, slowly and gently.

'Everything' is not lost, mistakes might be made but can be undone. As someone once said to me, 'You can't go back and make a new beginning but you can start again and make a new end.' Somewhere in these words that I know I don't quite remember correctly and somewhere in this day that's crept into night, amidst my own pain, stress, control, anger and fear, I do know that there is a happy unbroken me in arms' reach.

If I just hold onto this moment, embrace my feelings, hold myself close, remind myself that, even when my eyes can't see, my heart can feel, and I choose to feel all that is good, all that is positive. I can let go and know that

I am not alone. I'm just by myself from time to time and that's ok.

I might not have it all, in the way that 'all' is defined by so many, but what I have becomes nothing if I'm not grateful to 'be'. I open my eyes and I breathe deeply, I feel tired and I feel at ease and thank the world that I can see.

The writer recalls a childhood spent believing that it was normal to have an alcoholic parent.

Does it Ever Lose its Hold?

As a child growing up I never realised the impact of having an alcoholic parent. What did it mean? I thought it was normal to watch the clock on a Friday evening. The tension building, the dread and the sound of crying ringing in my ear – the Valium being reached for as a coping mechanism.

Door knocked. Was it the neighbour or a taxi dropping off from the pub?

Not fit to stand, falling flat on the face in the hall.

Dinner thrown in the bin.

Crying began . . .

Saturdays were quiet for a while – then it was like nothing had ever happened. Acceptance of behaviour, upset and the fact that little money was left to run the house with all the children was 'normal'.

I couldn't name it – secrecy was what was called for.

All I knew was to help with the chores and say nothing.

Hurtful things said, that I have carried all my life.

I'm listening to Frances Black singing 'Time':

> *'Time has taken all the pain out of your leaving*
> *And time has made it all much easier to bear*
> *I thought I would never get over those old feelings*
> *But time has made them fade away.'*

Such powerful words for pain so deep.

Drink stole my love and left emptiness within, that I have needed to rekindle.

Last year I went on a family programme on Rathlin Island. It was an amazing experience and a turning point. Memories were shared and strength developed within.

I remembered vividly how the AA came to my home one night when I was a teenager, to see if they could help. I had such high hopes that things might be ok.

It was a lovely evening outside; peace surrounded the fear. Time passed, stomach churned and yet nothing emerged.

They left – no words spoken – what did I do wrong to be ignored?

I distanced myself to find my way through and yet I know in my heart now as I mourn the loss, that I couldn't mend that broken heart.

I just needed someone to tell me that it was okay to talk about it.

I never knew I held that pain so long

I wrote the following poem in memory of that night:

Silence Speaks – From the Inside Out

Nerves, anticipation and fear
Door raps and strangers enter
Led out back into the unknown
Looking in through the glass
Don't know what to think or say!

Will it help?
Silence surrounds the space
Sweating hands
Counting minutes

Please let me know what's happening!
Door opens
Strangers appear
Don't tell me what I want to hear . . .
Say nothing at all!
Alone again to feel the pain
Why did it have to be this way?

*A man recalls how attending support
group meetings helped him to understand
his son's addiction.*

We had noticed big changes in our son for a while. The most notable was the terrible smell of stale alcohol when he got into my car at weekends. He was staying out until the early hours three or four nights a week and getting up later and later during the day. He was gradually avoiding study, always making excuses for doing badly in exams. He seemed to be in a haze with no focus and becoming detached. He was looking more and more pale, and gradually more and more bloated, putting on weight particularly in the stomach area. He had little interest in activities, apart from ones where there would be plenty of booze flowing. We were worried sick and I was worried that when he was out and drunk he was also taking drugs.

Our son is just a really, really nice person, very loving, thoughtful and gentle. Tall, handsome and with a great personality. However, we knew he was also shy and we thought perhaps some of the binge-drinking when out socialising with his friends was in order to cover up his social anxieties. He was very close to his mum and me, and I knew my wife's illness and medical restrictions were troubling him and taking their toll.

Following my wife's death, his drinking got worse. He was in his twenties, and went on major drink binges every weekend and even sometimes during the week. He had managed to qualify for social welfare benefits because of summer work he did while at secondary school and during the first few years at college. Basically, his life involved getting up in the afternoon or evening, going out with a few different sets of people, and drinking until he dropped. He pretended to be studying and attending college but we later found out he was not attending most classes and not sitting the exams.

Myself and my other children tried to talk to him and to persuade him to stop drinking. We held weekly meetings. We organised that he attend counselling and he went to several different counsellors. But he seemed to be getting worse. If we went to see a football match or to a live concert he would disappear shortly after the start and you would be sure to find him at the bar. He was admitted to hospital and other treatment centres for in-house treatment, and either drank during the course and was thrown out or drank a few days after being released from the programme.

In the meantime, myself and his siblings decided we needed help. We were finding empty spirit bottles, half-bottles, naggins of whiskey, gin, vodka, everything under his bed, in wardrobes, under his mattress, in the back shed, back garden, even the dog's kennel, not to mention the plastic bags filled with empty beer cans.

We got the name of a counsellor who had been well-recommended and together we visited him one gloomy Monday morning, not even a little optimistic that he could help. He was amazing: professional, knowledgable, expert and well-read on every aspect of addiction. It was clear that he had huge hands-on experience in assisting addicts.

When I went to that first meeting with him I felt we had a problem that could not be resolved. Now, for the first time, I had a reason for hope, real hope that maybe we could get clear-headed advice that would allow us help ourselves to cope with his problems and, most importantly, to help him.

Eventually, he went to see the counsellor and we knew after that meeting that he was impressed with this man's knowledge and experience, which gave him real hope that his life could be improved and that he could get off the terrible never-ending slippery slide. He was also confident that anything he discussed with the counsellor would be strictly confidential. I guess the counsellor was a conduit between him and the family, and that also helped.

After attending the counsellor for a few months I heard about a course to be held one night a week for ten weeks, organised by The RISE Foundation. My son continued to live at home with me and was continuing his drinking. We were all benefiting from the help and advice provided by the counsellor but I was feeling under strain and exhausted that he was still binge-drinking.

I went to my first RISE meeting at Wicklow Street not knowing what to expect, and not knowing whether I would attend the full course. I must admit I was sceptical as to whether the meetings could help. When I entered the meeting room I had a good positive feeling as I was met by one of the organisers who was friendly, relaxed and who introduced me to other people like myself who had joined the course. The main realisation during that first meeting was that all the other people seeking help and advice were experiencing problems arising from one of their loved ones having a major addiction. Fathers, mothers, brothers, sisters, sons, daughters – we're all going through the horrors of being addicted to alcohol or drugs or a combination of addictions, and the major adverse consequences for our families.

After each presentation, and a friendly chat with other participants over a cup of tea and biscuits, there was a group session where each of us talked about our own situation. It was harrowing to hear some of the stories but it was never a sad meeting because at all times we were being nudged forward with advice and suggestions from the two excellent counsellors, and the helpful and constructive advice of the other participants.

I am happy to say that although my son is not fully off alcohol, he now only occasionally falls off the wagon and manages to climb back on immediately. He took up a full-time job about a year ago and he has passed his exams. He enjoys his work and the achievement of not ever missing a day from work because of alcohol. He still has struggles but he is a different person. He looks great, has lost all the surplus pounds, lost the jowly look that he had when drinking. He and the family are now helping each other, and we are so much closer to each other having shared this experience.

A woman tells her husband how she turned a corner on coping with his addiction.

Let's be Honest with Myself

If I'm going to be honest I always knew you drank too much and had a problem. But, in a strange way, it was all very normal, very acceptable. We were young when we first met and had a great bunch of friends. We'd all meet up every weekend, and sometimes after work during the week too. We'd have a few . . . Why am I lying? . . . We'd have a lot to drink, and then sometimes move on to a club, then even later to Leeson Street to the late-night wine bars. Sometimes one of us would drive a few people home even though we were drunk. There were many mornings I'd wake up and I wouldn't know where I was or how I got home. so who am I to be preaching now, I suppose?

It was the same when we'd go abroad or spend weekends away at the races, sporting events or other festivals. We spent a lot of time drinking in between the gigs and games, and then spent the next day laughing and joking about the antics from the night before.

We were young with very few responsibilities. Our wedding day was just another big hooley but very enjoyable. I awoke in our honeymoon suite the next morning only to find that you were still in the lobby drinking with a few of the lads.

I suppose when I got pregnant that's when I started to really notice. I'd still go out with you to meet our friends and during the nine months we had two major celebrations to attend: the weddings of your best friend and my sister. I was adamant that I was not going to drink during my pregnancy. Sure, nine months was nothing to protect the health of our much-wanted baby. Little did I know then that I would never drink again. I thought that you might slow down a little too for moral support but instead you just started going to the pub more regularly without me and used me at weekends as your own private taxi.

I couldn't believe how loud you would get with drink on you. I could really see the changes. At your best friend's wedding. you made a complete show of yourself. He had chosen you to be his best man, and your speech was a total mess. You slurred your words and laughed at jokes that only you found funny – you were pissed and the meal hadn't even started. I was mortified. I said to one of my closest friends: 'Oh my God, he's locked. I don't know what has gotten into him lately.' But she wasn't surprised at all; instead she just said, 'Ah, it's because you're sober!' I just sat there, thinking, 'How could I have married such an idiot?' But she was completely right: this was the first time that I was not drunk with you. I would normally be tipsy myself by that point.

Through the two weddings, and much to my annoyance, my mortification, I got all the usual responses. 'Ah he's grand.' 'He's just enjoying himself.' 'Let him sleep it off there.' Much to my annoyance.

Ironically, very soon after, I was to have one of the worst

and best days of my life, when I had to drive myself to the hospital one night, in labour, because you had arrived home drunk. I gave birth to the most beautiful little girl on my own; I was too proud to call anyone to come with me. When your friend eventually brought you to the hospital you were only half-sober hours after the birth. I could still get the stale smell of drink and smoke off you. And then you went on another bender to celebrate the birth of our child.

So, as the years flew by, I just adapted to family life. We have two more beautiful children but we drifted further and further apart. I preferred to stay home with the kids and every evening you went to the pub after work. I would have the kids in bed early before you came home. The house was immaculate; I'd clean and re-clean like a lunatic. My nerves would not rest until I heard the car in the driveway, thanking God that yet again you hadn't been stopped on the way home. Sometimes, one of the lads would insist that they drop you back because they knew how important your licence was to your job.

I got on with the usual Mammy things: cooking, cleaning, lunches, ironing, washing, school runs, football, gymnastics and occasionally I'd bring the kids off on holidays to my sister's mobile home in Wexford for a little break. It's unbelievable how time flies by when you're rearing a family.

When the kids hit their teens, there was a huge change in our house. You embarrassed them in front of their friends, and they'd get angry with your attitude when you'd arrive home drunk. I started sounding like my mother: 'Ah, for pity's sake, just ignore him.' But I understood their frustrations. I tried to speak to you on many occasions about it but you just would not listen to me. You'd have all the excuses in the world – you worked hard, you were entitled to a drink; it's the kids, they're cheeky, you would never speak to your father like that; I had turned the kids against you. It still didn't stop the door-banging and arguing the next evening when it would start all over again.

I'd look at our friends doing things together with their kids, other fathers standing at the sidelines at the football matches on Sunday mornings, cheering on their sons, other parents in the playground. They must have all thought that I was a widow or a lone parent because I was always on my own.

I felt miserable, lonely, isolated and hurt, very hurt. I was beginning to feel feelings that I had buried away under that thick skin of mine for years. Through the kids' eyes I was beginning the see the real picture. Resentment was eating me up, I wasn't getting any younger and home life was getting really tough. One of our sons had begun to really rebel. He was getting into trouble and you weren't any support at all. I began to wonder if I should have left you years ago – staying together for the sake of the kids really wasn't working out at all.

During one of my many meetings with his school, the school counsellor asked me was everything all right at home. I just burst out crying and began to speak about how worried I was, how I was beginning to recognise just how dysfunctional our home life really was. No wonder he was getting into trouble – he was probably just as frustrated as me. I had been living in denial for a long, long time. After a very long first meeting with the counsellor, she was able to give me the numbers of some groups and people who could help.

I have just started on a new journey that's really helping me. I'm having to be open and honest about how I really feel. I'm getting stronger and I feel that very soon I will be able to face some of the toughest decisions in my life to date.

I haven't given up on you. I'm really hoping that the work I am doing on myself right now is going to help you to make changes in your life too. But I am preparing myself for the fact that I may have to go it alone for a while for the sake of my family and myself. I am beginning to lose the guilty feelings that have made me stick this out for so long, and regain some of the self-esteem I once had. I no longer walk this road alone but in the company of many people who have been here before and who understand how I feel.

As the serenity prayer goes: 'Every day I ask God to grant me the serenity to accept the things I cannot change, the courage to change the things I can, and the wisdom to know the difference.' This line alone has given me so much strength and hope.

Living in the Moment

'Present-moment living, getting in touch with your "now", is at the heart of effective living. When you think about it, there really is no other moment you can live. Now is all there is, and the future is just another present moment to live when it arrives. One thing is certain, you cannot live it until it does appear.'

Wayne Dyer

Whether in addiction, or living with addiction, negative or painful emotions, such as being sad, angry, lonely or resentful, are very prominent. These emotions, especially anger and resentment, often arise from an unresolved connection with something from our past. Unresolved resentments can be the number one cause of relapse for someone in recovery from addiction.

When someone we love is in addiction, fears about the future, near or distant, can also affect our emotions. For example: 'Are they going to come home tonight?' Or 'Will they kill themselves, or somebody else?' Of course this is natural under the circumstances. Family members may experience the same loss of self-esteem as the person in addiction. We can lose ourselves physically, emotionally and spiritually. It can lead to depression and anxiety, so it's critical we address the issues facing us before they cause irreparable harm.

By focusing on the now, instead of projecting into the future, we can eliminate the worry, fear and anxiety that comes from being preoccupied with the future. When in the now moment, we are no longer focused on the past, and emotional charges no longer have a hold over us.

Life unfolds in the present. So often, we can let the present slip away all too easily. But the reality is that we only have this present moment. We may have goals and visions for the future but only this moment exists. When we learn to step back and just allow this moment to be what it is, we open ourselves up to a new empowering reality.

We all have a divine purpose and that is to grow spiritually, make a distinct, loving contribution to this world, and realise that our thoughts are creating our lives. Many of us can neglect to use those thoughts in an empowering way. Now is the time to re-empower ourselves by living in the present moment. No more wanting or yearning for more, just the peace and joy of this moment that awaits us when we surrender to it. It is in this state of surrender that we will actually begin to see life.

American journalist and author Jim Bishop once said, 'Nothing is as far away as one minute ago.' Right here and right now is where our freedom is found. Life happens in this moment, and when we learn to accept that we become free from those things that hold us back.

If we wait to be happy sometime in the future, we might be waiting a very long time!

Frances

Singer Mick Flavin writes about his journey.

My Addiction Almost Ruined My Life

In February 2011, I celebrated 25 years alcohol free. Until then, drink was a central part of my life. I couldn't get enough of it. It's only looking back that I realise the effect it was having on me, my wife and family. Up until 1974, I was a casual drinker. That was the year I began playing music in pubs. It became the norm every weekend to stay on and get a drink when the gig was over. At the time I was also holding down a day job but, as things got progressively worse with the drinking, the weekend carried on into the weekdays and I began missing Mondays and Tuesdays. I carried on like this for a number of years. On several occasions I tried AA, which would lead me to quit for maybe a month at a time. But when I went back to the drink, I'd be worse than ever. Things got bad at home to the extent that Mary, my wife, left with the kids on a few occasions. Even this did not bring me to my senses. The only thing that really mattered to me was to be able to go out and drink and have a good time.

My GP advised me on several occasions to go and seek help, but I paid no heed. The lowest point in my drinking career happened when I went on a binge that lasted about three weeks, night and day. One night I came home to find no one was there. Mary had left with the kids, and, this time, it was clear she wasn't coming back. Reality hit home hard and I realised what drink was doing to me and my family. The next day, I went to my GP, who in turn advised me to seek help at the Alcoholic Unit in Mullingar. This I did. There I was advised to take up the seven-week therapy programme. Initially I was reluctant, but finally I got the courage to go ahead with it. I came back home after that programme and followed up with a two-year aftercare programme. That was 25 years ago and, thank God, I've never had a slip.

Thankfully, in time, the family got back together again, and it's hard to believe looking back that things could have got as bad as they did. Nowadays, we are happier than ever, with two lovely sons, daughters-in-law and grandchildren.

Mick Flavin

Appendix

Below is a list of useful resources/support organisations.

www.actionsuicide.ie

The Action on Suicide Alliance mission is to reduce the incidence of suicide and self-harm in Ireland by advocating the government provision of suicide-prevention measures and mental-health services.

www.addictionireland.ie

The National Drug Advisory and Treatment Centre (DTCB), established 1969, is the longest established treatment service in the country, providing effective, high-quality and client-focused caring professional treatment for those experiencing difficulties with substance abuse.

www.addictivebehaviours.com

This website offers help and information for those struggling with gambling, food and sexual addiction.

www.aisieri.ie

This service offers a confidential and professional treatment programme for those experiencing difficulties with alcohol, substance abuse and gambling.

www.aislinn.ie

Aislinn is a recovery centre providing drug-free addiction treatment for people between 15 and 21 years of age.

www.al-anon-ireland.org

Al-Anon offers peer-to-peer understanding and non-professional support for families and friends of problem drinkers in an anonymous environment, whether the person in addiction is still drinking or not.

www.alcoholicsanonymous.ie

Alcoholics Anonymous is a fellowship of men and women who share their experience, strength and hope with each other so that they may solve their common problem and help others to recover from alcoholism.

www.alcoholireland.ie

Alcohol Action Ireland is the national charity for alcohol-related issues. It's vision is of an Ireland that recognises and challenges the harm caused by alcohol.

www.alcoholresponse.com

Alcohol Response Ireland is a genuine civil society effort to provide practical help in tackling Ireland's chronic alcohol problem.

www.ascert.biz

ASCERT empowers people to make a positive difference where alcohol and drug related issues damage lives. Ascert, Bridge Street, Lisburn, County Antrim.

www.aware.ie

Aware's mission is to create a society where people with depression and their families are understood and supported, are free from stigma and have access to a broad range of appropriate therapies to enable them to reach their full potential.

www.barnardos.ie and www.barnardos.org.uk

With more than 40 community-based centres, national services and links with partner organisations, Barnardos delivers programmes to help as many children and their families as they can.

www.bodywhys.ie

Bodywhys is the Eating Disorders Association of Ireland. It offers support, information and understanding for people with eating disorders, their families and friends.

www.bushypark.ie

BushyPark Treatment Centre is a 13-bed, residential treatment centre located in 17 acres of parkland, 3 miles outside Ennis Town. The centre offers a 28-day residential programme for people addicted to alcohol, drugs and gambling based on the 12-step philosophy/Minnesota Model of treatment.

www.carlislehouse.org

Carlisle House is a residential substance misuse treatment centre situated near the centre of Belfast. It caters for individuals from 18 to 65 years, from the greater Belfast and North Antrim area. Carlisle House also welcomes private clients.

www.citizensinformation.ie

The Citizens Information Board is the statutory body which supports the provision of information, advice and advocacy on a broad range of public and social services.

www.clarecare.ie

Clare Care provides information, counselling and treatment for those in addiction.

www.console.ie

Console is a national organisation providing professional counselling, support and helpline services to those bereaved through suicide.

www.drinkthinkproject.org

The Drink Think Project aims to protect children from alcohol-related harm in the Derry City Council area.

www.drugs.ie

Drugs.ie provides information on alcohol and drugs. It is funded by the Health Service Executive and managed by Crosscare Drug and Alcohol Programme.

www.eatingdisorders.ie

The eating disorder resource centre of Ireland provides a wide range of information on eating disorders.

www.fasaonline.org

A Belfast-based group focusing on the promotion of drug and suicide awareness.

www.forest.ie

A residential treatment centre for a wide range of addictions situated in County Wicklow.

www.gamblersanonymous.ie

Gamblers Anonymous is a fellowship of men and women who share their experience, strength and hope with each other, so that they may solve their common problem and help others to recover from gambling addiction.

www.thehanlycentre.com

The Hanly Centre provides counselling for alcohol- and substance abuse-related problems.

www.hopehouse.ie

Hope House in County Mayo offers residential treatment and aftercare support to those suffering from alcohol and substance abuse and compulsive gambling.

www.hse.ie

The Health Services Executive is responsible for providing health and personal social services for everyone living in the Republic of Ireland.

www.hurt.org.uk

Hurt, is a unique, holistic drop-in centre, based in Derry, offering holistic approaches to addiction rehabilitation.

www.icapni.org

ICAP's mission is to set young people, caught in substance misuse, free from their addiction, and to provide ongoing support to them and their families.

www.nacd.ie

The National Advisory Committee on Drugs advises the government on problem drug use in Ireland in relation to prevalence, prevention, consequences and treatment, based on analysis and interpretation of research findings.

www.na-ireland.org

Narcotics Anonymous is a non-profit fellowship of men and women who share their experiences in order to help themselves and others to overcome their problems with drug use.

www.nicas.info

Addiction NI is a part of the Northern Ireland Community Addiction Service, a registered charity providing treatment and support for people who are dependent on alcohol or drugs.

www.northlands.org.uk

Helps individuals, families and communities to understand and deal with the many issues that contribute to problems with alcohol, drug, gambling and other addictive behaviours in the context of each individual's situation.

www.rehabclinic.org.uk

Rehab Clinic is part of Panacea UK, a dedicated team of healthcare experts who are well-respected in the industry, providing information on treatment centres in Northern Ireland and the UK.

www.therisefoundation.ie

The RISE Foundation is a charity that supports families who have loved ones in addiction.

www.rutlandcentre.ie

The Rutland Centre is a registered charity founded in 1978 which has since grown to become the largest and most respected private addiction rehabilitation centre in Ireland.

www.samaritans.org

The Samaritans provide confidential, non-judgemental emotional support, 24 hours a day, for people who are experiencing feelings of distress or despair.

www.suicideorsurvive.ie

Suicide or Survive is an organisation and therapy provider dedicated to removing the stigma associated with mental health and suicide prevention.

www.taborlodge.ie

Tabor Lodge is a treatment centre for those having difficulties with alcohol, drugs, gambling, food as well as a variety of other addictions. It was established by The Sisters of Mercy in 1989.

www.talbotgrove.ie

Talbot Grove is a treatment centre in Castleisland, County Kerry that provides a 30-day residential, addiction-treatment programme, aftercare and family/concerned persons' programmes.

www.toranfieldhouse.ie

Toranfield House is a newly established residential addiction treatment centre in County Wicklow. They are committed to caring for people and their families struggling to free themselves from addiction.

www.whiteoaksrehabcentre.com

White Oaks is a treatment centre, based in County Donegal, for people in addiction.

www.womensaid.ie

Women's Aid is a leading national organisation that has been working to address the issue of domestic violence in Ireland for more than 35 years.

www.3ts.ie

3Ts (Turn the Tide of Suicide) is a registered charity, founded to raise awareness of the problem of suicide in Ireland and to raise funds to help lower suicide rates through dedicated research, educational support and intervention.

www.12steptreatmentcentres.com

12 Step Treatment Centres are based in the UK and have registered many addiction treatment, drug treatment, drug abuse treatment, alcohol abuse treatment, addiction rehabs, drug rehabs, alcohol rehabs, plus other related facilities in the 12 Step Treatment Centres guide.

Treatment agencies for alcohol and drug misuse.

These are too numerous to list but advice can be received from your local GP or primary care centre, from national helplines and from the HSE or NHS.

Acknowledgements

I am deeply appreciative of all the people who have so generously contributed to the book and who have so kindly taken the time to write their stories, poems and pieces with such honesty, sincerity and feeling. It is not the easiest task to speak or write about addiction, and the impact that it can have on our friends, loved ones and family members. You should be very proud that your contribution will help others who are struggling to survive the impact of addiction and are on their own journey to recovery. For the protection of our loved ones, most of the pieces will remain anonymous, but you all know who you are and I want to thank you from the bottom of my heart. This is your book.

I would also like to thank so much the named contributors – Mary Coughlan, Ben Dunne, Mick Flavin, Rachael Keogh, Jimmy MacCarthy, Paul McGrath, Oisín McConville and Paddy Creedon – who have been so brave to speak about their own addiction in the past and now in our book. By doing so, you are also helping to break the shame and stigma attached to addiction and will hopefully encourage other people to seek the help they need.

I would also like to thank some people without whom this book would not have been possible. Thanks to Ciara Considine from Hachette Books Ireland for believing in the idea for this book and for working so hard to get it out in such a short time frame. To Pamela Doyle Woods who was absolutely brilliant in gathering all the material, and the rest. To Mark O'Doherty for all your hard work, patience and dedication. To Trish Morrissey for giving us the inspiration to do this. To Rabia Tabassum for your dedication, and to Fiona Sexton and Jennifer Nesbit. To Stephen Rowen and Irene Sherry for all their support through everything. To all at Social Entrepreneurs Ireland, Drury Communications and the team at Boys and Girls Advertising. To Jerry Kennelly from Killorglin and Marek Wystepek from Getty Images. To all at Hachette Books, especially Breda, Margaret and Joanna. To Brian for everything.

Thank you all so much.

Love,
Frances x